I/T
Architecture
in
Action

I/T Architecture in Action

in

Action

Bridging Business and I/T Strategies

RICHARD J. REESE

To order additional copies of this book, contact:
Xlibris Corporation
1-888-795-4274
www.Xlibris.com
Orders@Xlibris.com
42223

Dedication

For my wife Alla—the definition of style, strength, intelligence, and beauty; and for my children, for understanding my passion for work and my time-consuming hobbies.

Thanks to Meg Zold. Her editing and consultative expertise made this project a success.

Inspiration

For everyone who made a difference in my professional life or contributed to the concepts presented within, I thank you.

Kent Anderson, Howard Atlas, Greg Berkley, Chirayu Dave, Karen Davis, Dave Dillon, Doug Faist, Eoin Flannery, Paul Goodine, John Hayward, Ron Hirasawa, John Joseph, Steve Kagan, Paul Kleinman, Chris Koehler, Aldo Mancini, Dan McCue, Keith Nielsen, Diane Offereins, George Rimnac, Dan Sadler, Tom Schmitt, Glenn Schneider, Greg Stack, Andy Thomas, Keith Tobler, Dennis Waldron.

DISCLAIMER OF WARRANTY AND LIMITATION OF LIABILITIES

The information within this book is presented *as is* with no warranties regarding use by individuals or corporations. It represents general concepts and information available in the public domain and is not indicative of any particular intent to endorse or validate use or application thereof, by any individual or corporation mentioned within. Every effort has been made to make this book as complete and accurate as possible. Neither the publisher, nor the author, shall have liability to any person or entity with respect to any losses or damages, whether such losses and/or damages are construed as direct or consequential, resulting from use or reliance on the content herein. Discover Financial Services and all of its affiliates do not endorse this work; the contents do not reflect the views, opinions, or proprietary and/or confidential information of Discover Financial Services nor its affiliates, vendors, and partners. Comments regarding products mentioned within are the opinion of the author and have not been endorsed by the companies producing or marketing the products.

CONTENTS

LIST OF FIGURES

LIST OF TABLES

FOREWORD

As executive vice president and chief technology officer for a large financial institution, and as a member of the company's management committee, I see technology as a business driver. Yes, I/T's role is supporting the business. However, in the fast paced, highly competitive financial industry, maintaining a strategic focus is critical. Over my years in business, I have seen many attempts to apply standardization and process to I/T. While these efforts did provide improvements in the short term, over the long term, time-to-market and agility were sacrificed.

Technology standards and processes are key ingredients to running a good I/T unit and no reasonable person would debate the point. Too often, however, the overall culture of the company is not taken into account. Application of rigor in the wrong context leads to a larger organization structure and slow-to-market results. My experience is that a balance between strict rigor and organic innovation works best. The book you are about to read, *I/T Architecture in Action*, describes this balance. The author, Richard J. Reese, has worked for decades perfecting the techniques described in the following chapters. He has done a fine job of blending his own experience with industry trends and facts in a book that is not too technical yet will appeal to technicians. As he says, this is a management book about technology, not a technology book that touches on management.

Diane Offereins
EVP/CTO
Discover Financial Services

CHAPTER 1

Enterprise Architecture

Working within the information technology (I/T) function of a large enterprise can sometimes feel like being a crew member of a ship stranded in turbulent seas. With no strategic plans and outdated navigational tools, the crew has little chance of making it to safety. As soon as the wind direction changes, the boat is expected to turn quickly to avoid being swamped in a wave of change. The crew makes countless attempts to outmaneuver the storm and to respond to the turbulent conditions. However, the lack of strategic planning and investment in modern technology can result in a crew that is unable to guide the ship to its destination.

More than ever before, executive management is systems-aware and understands the value of systemic thinking. However, there remains a gulf between business strategy and I/T's ability to deliver the baseline infrastructure needed to facilitate change. This book describes what "enterprise architecture" is and why having such a function is a critical success factor in execution on business strategy.

The book acts as a bridge between those who think about business strategy and those who think about the technology necessary to achieve financial success. This work is unlike others written about the topic of systems architecture. Others tend to focus on how to *build* a systems architecture. Why not a book about what the architecture *is* and how it can help a business become more flexible and competitive? This is a management

1

book about technology, not a technology book that touches on management. Important technical concepts are described but not in such detail as to detract from the overriding message that enterprise architecture provides business flexibility.

This book provides a cross sectional view into how enterprise architecture can be a driving factor in medium to large size businesses. Most topics are introduced through a brief history of the technology, followed by enough description of the technical details to establish a context. Key terms are defined, and many of the definitions and other facts represented are cited through references.

While technical accuracy is an important tenet, the concepts behind the examples are more important. Where appropriate, the reader is invited to seek additional information. Technical topics are described to the level of detail necessary to bring the overriding concept into the forefront. Much of the content of this book has been derived from "feet on the street" experiences at companies like United Airlines, IBM, Discover Card (Discover Financial Services), Sears, Whirlpool Corporation, W.W. Grainger Inc., and others. The resulting work is a blend of technical facts combined with practical know-how that informs and educates.

Enterprise Architecture Defined

At a recent holiday party hosted by a leading systems architecture consulting company, a guest was asking, *"So what is system architecture, and what does a systems architect do? Does a systems architect program computers? My daughter is a computer programmer, is that what you do too?"* Well, those aren't such bad questions. To someone unfamiliar with technology, it's kind of hard to understand any job in I/T other than programming or fixing hardware.

To put the answer in perspective, many large companies are spending between $500MM and $1B on I/T budgets. At least 20 percent of these budgets are composed of management costs. That equates to between $10MM and $20MM, just in management "overhead." What intelligent businessperson would spend tens of millions on management without a plan? Take the construction industry, for example. Construction companies wouldn't even fund the start of a new building without an architect's building plan. How else could the builder determine if construction loans were of the correct size and if the building has a chance of being completed on time and within budget?

So then, why is it that many large enterprises don't have a formal systems architecture function or formal systems architects in place? Why don't more executive managers consult with key technology experts within the enterprise before launching new business initiatives or acquiring other companies? The answers to these questions are based on the legacy of I/T. Since the days of the "glass house" when mainframes were only used to run accounting and payroll applications, upper management has seen I/T as a cost center. Not all companies use I/T to improve operations effectiveness alone. Some also use I/T to position their business strategically. One good example of strategic use of technology is at United Parcel Service (UPS).

Back in the mid-1990s, UPS began working on wireless data access, computer pads, and handwriting recognition software. These efforts were targeted at improving the productivity of its vast delivery workforce. The baseline premise was that by improving the information available to the delivery agent, more packages could be delivered per agent per day. While it took UPS years to perfect the application and gain a positive payback on its investment, today the technology has been completely integrated into the daily delivery process not only at UPS, but at FedEx and others as well.

By linking data collected with a tablet device to the company Internet site, customer service is offloaded from call centers directly to the customer. Were these results intended when the project got underway in 1994? The web was barely on the minds of most business people in 1994. However, the introduction of a set of new technologies and their ultimate merge into a mainstream business process formed a brand new value stream for the customer and the company. The original vision of enhancing the productivity of the delivery workforce ended up being the new ante into a higher stakes game of customer self-service. How would any national or international overnight delivery business compete without such technology today?

In our example, did the business system come from the architecture, or did the architecture emerge from the business system? One can only look into the minds of those working on the initial stages of the project in 1993-94 to answer that question. However, the final solution that we are so familiar with today arose from a series of innovations that ranged from implementation of cellular towers, to improved portable computer battery life, to data compression routines and better panel displays. All of these form the architecture of the solution including software, databases, networks, hardware, and support personnel. Bringing all these elements together into a complete solution that actually works for business is the role of the *systems architect*. The specification of the particular components and how they interact with each other is the *systems architecture*.

An *I/T system architecture is the specification of components which form an information technology-based business solution. When the architecture spans business functions within a company, it is enterprise system architecture.* This definition of systems architecture is by no means exact. Major businesses and I/T functions tend to define the term to fit their own particular needs. Some think of architecture as "standards." Examples include standard software, network protocols, and hardware platforms. Some think of blueprints or plans for innovation. Others think of procedures and rules managed by a "governance body" within an enterprise. Depending on the organization, the architecture group might even be responsible for research and development activities for emerging technologies. The architecture function within the enterprise is all these things. Which functions are performed and which artifacts are produced, typically depends on the emphasis placed by the chief information officer (CIO).

If the CIO is driven by cost containment, the architecture function will be focused on standards, governance, and measurement of total cost of ownership (TCO). If the CIO is trying to drive innovation for business growth, architecture will be aimed at blueprints and R&D activities. Systems architecture exists whether it is formalized or not. It is present in the technology

4

purchased, developed and implemented by the enterprise over time. A novel way to view the existing technical footprint of an organization is as a reflection of technology decisions made over time. A quick look across the organization at the software, networks, databases, and computer hardware in use represents a tangible historical record of each and every technical decision.

Were these decisions made according to some strategy or "grand plan" or were they made one-by-one as immediate business needs dictated? When technology was brought in, were there plans to evolve and eventually retire it? Did the enterprise leverage its buying power, or was the technology purchased many times from the same vendor by different parts of the company? Was the solution sold to management as "throw away" or tactical, but is still in use five years later? How many interfaces were developed between systems in a point-to-point style over the years, and how many people support these today? By looking at the current state of systems architecture, much can be learned about how the enterprise makes decisions and funds technology projects. If the business is concerned about these questions and has no one to turn to for answers, then there is a need for the architecture function at the enterprise level.

The Case for Enterprise Architecture

Sometimes it's much easier to understand why something is necessary by looking at what life would be like without it. Let's paint a picture of a large enterprise of about $1B in sales revenue, with a net profit of about $100MM, or 10 percent. Such an enterprise might have around three hundred or so I/T employees, with I/T annual spend of 8 percent of sales, or $80MM. Now let's assume there are the standard business functional areas in place like sales, marketing, accounting, finance, human resources, production, planning, I/T, and purchasing. To complicate matters a bit, let's assume there are four product lines, and each line is managed as a profit center. There are discrete planning, sales, accounting, and some I/T functions within each profit center, but these share common services offered by the enterprise. A picture of such an enterprise structure would look like the following figure.

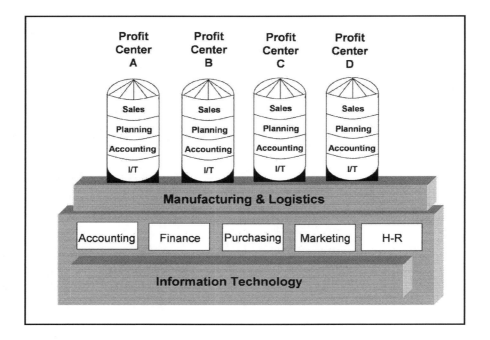

Figure 1—Sample Enterprise Structure

The fact that each line of business is modeled like a silo is no accident. This organization structure is quite typical of today's complex enterprise. Vice presidents are responsible for the profitability of their individual business unit, and they rely on shared functions provided by the corporate groups. Whether they pay for these functions or not is usually a matter of accounting policy. Whether they do pay for them at the unit cost level or via general allocations is an important issue for anyone working on standardization and reuse of common services.

Issues associated with having both distributed and centralized functions are not really unique to the I/T discipline. Accounting has been run this way for years across distributed multinational enterprises. The accountancy profession, however, is lucky to have standards bodies in place like Financial Accounting Standards Board (FASB) and others, to make sure financial results are reported using the same rules from silo to silo. What standards bodies exist for making sure I/T conducts operations the same way from silo to silo? Who will conduct audits and assure they are operating within standards and company policies? Is I/T accountable to the outside financial community like the accounting function?

By studying the sample business model, one can imagine all sorts of conflicts of interest associated with the I/T function. The examples in the table below amplify the need for a control process:

Conflict	*Who is Impacted*	*Consequences*
Each unit wants its own Internet Website.	Profit center, corporate groups, customers.	Brand image confusion, redundant web infrastructures, higher support costs.
Each unit attempts to sell to the same customer base.	Profit center, production dept., customers.	Redundant customer files, inaccurate and out of synch customer data, production priorities are in conflict.
Individual units negotiate with I/T vendors and procure software and hardware.	Profit center, corporate groups, vendors.	Lost buyer leverage, higher corporate I/T support costs, profit centers underestimate support resources.
Units each build electronic connections to large customers and suppliers.	Profit center, customers, suppliers.	Varying messaging protocols, security rules vary across the supply chain.

Table 1—Sample Conflicts of Interest

The table above shows how semiautonomous business units and corporate functions struggle for the use of scarce resources. Units are established to optimize their own bottom lines, while corporate functions strive to leverage capital investment and human resources across the whole organization. This sets up a natural conflict of interest in the absence of a control group.

Enter the *enterprise architecture function*. If performed correctly, the function sets up win-win scenarios between the conflicting goals of disparate business units and the corporate service entity. By establishing the ground rules for engagement, entities across the enterprise will know their boundaries and are able to operate freely within them. How this is done without slowing down the enterprise is described in chapter 2. But helping to bridge conflicting priorities is only one aspect of the enterprise architecture function.

A mature architecture function is positioned to use its corporate stature strategically. By matching business strategy with technical direction, wrapped with I/T standards, upper management has its hands on the controls of the entire enterprise. By managing the financial side (as they have always done) and leveraging long term technology plans, upper management can cause change to happen at the enterprise level. Chapter 3 explores how this is done in a proactive style, making the I/T function the driver for change across the enterprise, instead of I/T trying to react and play catch-up with management direction.

The Architecture Maturity Curve

How can the enterprise architecture function grow from simply acting as the "standards police" to serving as the lever of strategic change? Figure 2 below identifies a typical progression. Where a particular architecture function exists on the curve is dependent on a number of factors. These include the size of the I/T organization, the understanding by senior management of the value I/T creates, whether the company has a "fast follower" strategy or "market leader" strategy within its industry and, to some extent, the health of the company's industry and the economy in general.

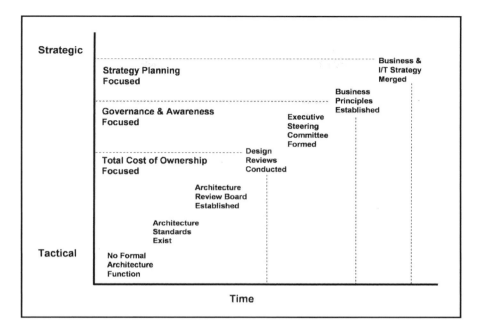

Figure 2—Architecture Maturity Curve

As figure 2 shows, the focus changes over time as the function becomes more mature. Maturity in this case is measured by the degree to which the enterprise architecture function is connected with senior management. In the beginning, the function is seen as a necessity to good management practices within the I/T community. As time progresses, and with great effort on the part of some key leaders within I/T, an executive steering committee is formed. At first, the steering committee will focus on assuring that governance of standards and procedures is working. Later, the steering committee will find value-added benefits from gaining a view across operations as presented by the architecture function.

As the process matures, the business and I/T will collaborate on producing a set of principles. These principles help both the business and I/T make judgment calls about conflicting priorities and technology direction across the enterprise. Once principles are well established and understood by key management, the

9

collaborative planning process causes I/T and the business to blend from a new product development perspective.

Take care not to pass judgment about being low on the curve. It may be perfectly fine for an enterprise to focus on governance and TCO with an architecture function. A mature business with a stable market share, or a business unit designed to be a "cash cow" might not have to link I/T planning with business planning so tightly. I/T's function in such a scenario is keeping the lid on costs and assuring high availability and stability of systems. A startup business or an enterprise that must reinvent itself will have to move up the curve quickly or face the chaotic introduction of technologies. The chaotic adoption of technologies can go unnoticed and even be seen as a positive strategy, (aka., the first mover advantage associated with "dot com" start-ups in the late 1990s) until heavy cost burdens overtake the speed-to-market advantages.

This classic trade-off between being fast and flexible and controlled and cost-efficient represents a significant problem for senior management. Quite often, the very managers needing to be fast and flexible within their department also rely on shared stable operating platforms for the core business. Faced with market pressures, line-of-business mangers almost always come down on the side of speed and flexibility over cost-effectiveness. There can be three to five years of "rope" extended to them in the form of acceptable losses on the books as they build a new brand or business.

However, there comes a day when the unit cannot sustain itself with inefficient processes and is in need of the structure provided by standards and commonality of procedures and systems infrastructure. In our hypothetical silo example, should each profit center build its own network? How about having individual data centers? A case could be made for one or two profit centers if they are very successful. However, there will also be those units without the economies of scale to support themselves. The following figure shows that there is going be a "day of reckoning" for units that assume they can stand alone, without paying attention to what is shared and what is truly unique to a unit.

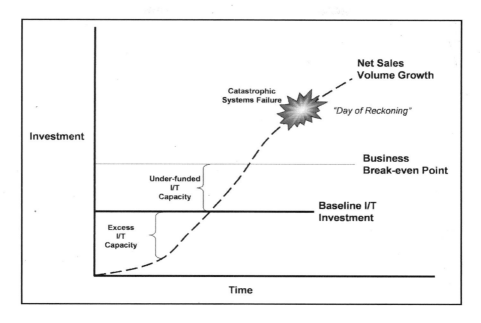

Figure 3—EA Investment Model

Figure 3 is a bit complex. However, it shows in graphic form what can happen if I/T investment in capacity is not matched with the business plan. The dashed line indicates growth in sales volume over time. Major I/T investments take place periodically, and with each investment the I/T cost basis goes up. In this case, to become profitable, no additional investments are made. For a new business, sales volume tends to start slow, and after management effort and other investments kick in, sales start to pick up rapidly. They will rise quickly until they begin to grow linearly in most cases, following the traditional product life cycle.

What can happen if management is not investing in technology to improve worker productivity? A false sense of security about baseline cost is developed in the minds of senior managers. In an effort to drive toward the break-even point and make business plans work, management may be tempted to hold off on investing in new technologies. The risk here is waiting until after the break-even point is reached; if sales actually do take off (the day of reckoning), there are no industrial strength systems to support the business volume.

This happened to a few web-based businesses around the year 2000 as they did not invest ahead of the coming demand. This also happens in the telecommunications industry if bandwidth has been under funded. Matching the growth curve in the business to the technical capacity available at any point in time is the job of a mature enterprise architecture function. Without discipline, the organization is left with the only viable option, overspending on capacity each year. Those who don't overspend tend to get caught in a "productivity trap" and rely on adding to the workforce or incurring losses in the form of less-worker productivity. In a small business or a profit center, this can be disastrous, but in a large enterprise the consequences are not as readily apparent. Inefficiency due to reliance on outdated technology or manual processes can eat away at the bottom line for years.

Chapter 1—Summary

This chapter defined *enterprise architecture* and made a case for the function in larger companies. The author used an example of wireless computing to demonstrate systems architecture and how it evolved from an idea to a complete business solution. Once establishing a definition for enterprise architecture, a hypothetical company structure was used to identify the need for a company-wide governance process. An enterprise architecture maturity model was presented. The model described how a typical architecture function can evolve within a business. The chapter then explored what can happen if investments in technology are out of synchronization with business growth patterns. The inevitable "day of reckoning" may come if capacity is under funded in pursuit of reaching profit targets.

The following chapter explores the process of merging business strategy planning with I/T strategy planning via *principle-based architecture*. Business strategy planning and I/T strategy planning processes are defined, and the concept of using architecture principles to manage behavior is introduced. The chapter concludes with presenting sample architecture principles.

CHAPTER 2

Principle-Based Architecture

Our crew lost at sea needs instruments to help them find their way. Without instruments and the ability to communicate with others along the journey, they will have a tough time making it to land. I/T can try to determine where the business is heading but going it alone is risky. What tools are available to match business plans with I/T plans? Once plans are matched, how can they be maintained together as day-to-day decisions are made? Is merging plans and then keeping them synchronized, even possible in such a fast-paced, ever-changing business climate?

This chapter covers business and I/T strategy planning at a high level. A methodology for merging business and I/T strategic plans is presented, and a process for keeping them in sync is described. The chapter closes with defining how *principle-based architecture* acts as the "invisible hand" to affect decisions and management behavior regarding technology across the enterprise.

Business Strategy Planning

Many books already exist about strategy planning for business. Therefore, this book touches on the aspect of the overall process that relates to I/T planning and how enterprise architecture plays a role in the planning process. First, I/T management must understand that the key word here is *strategy*. Strategy differs markedly from *tactics*, and this difference must be understood by I/T management in order to define systems architecture at the enterprise level.

Strategic thinking is really a series of moves, like how a good chess player plans many moves ahead, aimed at a positive planned outcome. Strategic planning establishes a format for making decisions and investments that position a firm for the long term. Sometimes, the moves may seem disjoint or even stupid to those not involved in defining the strategy, but once all the moves have been played out, the strategy becomes apparent. Tactics, on the other hand, have to do with execution of plans. Sometimes, a tactical decision is made which may deviate from the overall plan, but if everyone is aware of the strategy, they will have an easier time accepting a short term deviation in direction.

Business strategy can be a complex topic; however, a simplified view of business model strategy is shown in the following figure.

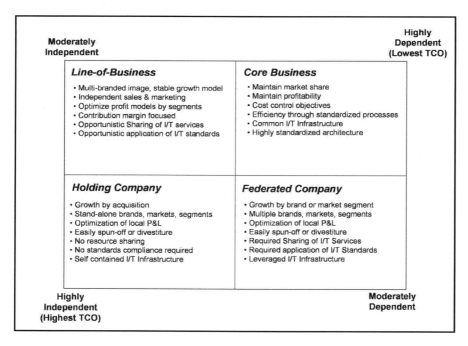

Figure 4—Business Strategy Matrix

The model in figure 4 shows how a business can be organized to reach its overarching growth goals. The *holding company model* is characterized by being highly independent from whatever corporate functions exist. By definition, a business organized as a holding company only cares about the value of its subsidiaries. Value is measured by financial metrics such as return on assets, or return on shareholder equity. To gain market share, additional companies could be acquired. If a particular company is unprofitable or is determined to be detrimental to the financial objectives of the parent company, it can be quickly disposed of. In this model, even successful companies can be disposed of if their market value is greater than the growth potential, or return on assets, to the parent company. Subsidiaries are usually completely autonomous, both physically and procedurally, from their holding company parent.

The *line-of-business model* is used for entities that are somewhat like the holding company model, but the corporate entity has more control over the brand image and target market. Since lines of business strive to maximize sales and profits of their particular product mix, they tend to share infrastructure with the corporate core. As long as a line of business contributes to fund the fixed cost base of the enterprise as a whole, it may be allowed to operate, even at a financial bottom line loss. Over time, lines of businesses tend to migrate toward another quadrant. They will either be very successful and become more independent or be less successful and be more dependent on the core business.

The *core business model* focuses on driving a successfully profitable business to be more profitable through continuous process improvements, resulting in higher productivity. Productivity is measured by the efficiency of the business processes in place to drive sales and reduce operating costs. Core businesses are usually highly dependent on common business processes and the economies of scale associated with investments in tried-and-true practices and markets. Core businesses tend to stay at steady state and experience revenue growth in the single digits over the long term until some major market forces change within their industry.

The *federated model* is characterized by businesses having independent operating units but working according to a set of standards that have been established by the corporate core. A good example here is a franchise operation. Such businesses are free to operate within their geographic or market groupings and could also leverage multiple brands within the target market area. They tend to establish their own business processes within their coverage area and need to interact frequently with the corporate core as resources need to be replenished.

So how does the four-quadrant model relate to business strategy? Senior management selects an operating model even if they haven't formally named the strategy. For the core business model, executives focused on cost control and maintaining the position within their industry will make investment decisions to improve business processes and cut costs. Any large company with a single or predominant operating model fits this strategic profile.

For the line-of-business model, executives focused on market segment penetration and autonomy will try and break away from the "mother ship" with their line of business. They "want their cake and eat it too" by being independent but still leveraging common services provided by the core of the corporation. A good example here would be Procter & Gamble. Each major brand is run independently from the other. However, core company services are shared.

For the federated model, executives charged with running entire sub-companies while leveraging a consistent brand image, will stay in line with corporate standards and directives. Think of the various divisions of General Motors. They are all GM but run their own operations. It's a federation of businesses.

In the holding company model, a senior management team may choose to stay at arm's length from the companies they own. They may simply monitor the financial progress of each firm and build a portfolio of businesses. Each business might be totally independent in every way from the other. Think of the Altria Group. At one time, the parent company owned both Philip Morris and Kraft Foods. The strategy of the holding company model is to maximize income and avoid economic down turns through diversification.

I/T Strategy Planning

Of course I/T groups within large enterprises do strategic planning. There have been books and methodologies published on how to do long term strategy planning for the I/T function. This book is about systems architecture. Therefore, the focus is on how I/T strategy can be integrated with business strategy and how the underlying systems architecture relates to the coordinated strategic plans.

So what is I/T strategy planning in the context of enterprise architecture, and how does it tie into business strategy planning? I/T management develops its own strategic plans. These plans should be based on a combination of what is possible from a technological perspective over the next planning horizon and how the business intends to focus its resources over the same time period. By reviewing the project portfolio of each business operating unit, I/T should have insight into where the most significant structural changes will be required. To extend the I/T planning horizon far into the future, technology research and I/T industry trends can be incorporated into the planning process through the I/T research and development process. Figure 5 graphically shows how the planning processes are integrated.

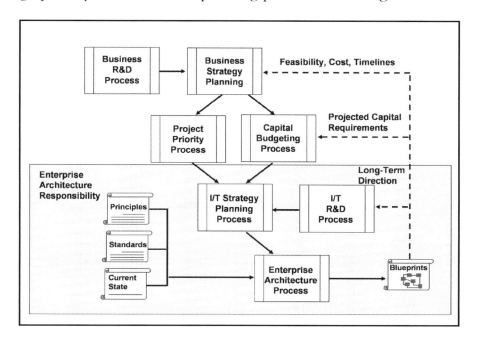

Figure 5—I/T Strategy Planning Process

The entire process is iterative and can be run as often as an organization wishes to update its master plans. Important links between the business and I/T planning functions are the *project priority list* and *capital budget plan*. These artifacts are essential to making sure that I/T "gets it right" when it comes to making decisions having a long term impact to the direction of the enterprise. Since both of these artifacts are unique to each company, there is no need to describe their formats here.

A list of new projects must be produced and approved by upper management for the planning process to be effective. The list need not be in priority sequence for the I/T planning process to get underway. This is true because whether the I/T planning process considers human and financial resource constraints, or not, is up to the planning team to consider. If the I/T strategic plan is expected to be implemented in the business planning horizon, then a basic set of priorities are necessary. However, these priorities need not always trade one project for another. A good I/T strategy plan should enable a group of business projects that would otherwise not be feasible on a one-by-one basis.

The way the business decides to spend money over time is a great indicator of where it believes its priorities are. Therefore, by reviewing the capital budget plan, I/T can gain great insight into the future direction of the business. In addition, to enable various business projects, I/T must be able to influence how the business deploys capital resources. Therefore, the capital budget plan is a key input to the I/T strategy planning process, as well as the enterprise architecture planning process.

The enterprise architecture planning process consists of combining the inputs from the business with I/T strategy plans and developing a more detailed and technical view. Enterprise architecture adds its own inputs to the planning process. These are *architecture principles*, *architecture standards*, and the *current state* of the enterprise architecture. The key output from the enterprise architecture planning process are "white papers" that go to domain architects.

Domain Architects are people skilled in technology infrastructure who have knowledge of industry trends and direction within their particular domain of expertise. Domain architects use the white papers and industry trends as inputs to formulate the architectural blueprint for the enterprise.

An *architecture blueprint* is a set of documents that identify how technology and I/T strategy plans will affect the five major constructs of enterprise architecture. These constructs are application architecture, information architecture, network architecture, platform architecture and operations management architecture. These areas are described in detail later beginning with chapter 4. The architecture blueprint is then expressed in various formats and used by senior executives to determine feasibility of business proposals as they relate to I/T.

Architectural Models

The unique characteristics of the four business strategies described in figure 4 relate directly to I/T strategies. For example, it would not make much sense for I/T to try to build a common customer database for a holding company. Building a common customer database may not even be the correct thing to do given a line-of-business strategy and operating model. However, both the core business and, to some extent, the federated model could benefit from the consistency of information that a common customer database can offer. There are specific characteristics of the enterprise systems architecture that can be associated with the strategy and organizational model selected by the senior management team. The table below describes these characteristics.

Strategic Model	Business Characteristics	Architectural Characteristics
Holding Company	Growth by acquisition Stand-alone business processes and product brands	• Stand-alone systems are used. • Few online interfaces with corporate systems are available. Systems are not directly integrated across various business units.

Strategic Model	Business Characteristics	Architectural Characteristics
	Stand-alone assets Corporate consolidates financials Ease of divestiture	• Stand-alone networks with firewalls between network segments exist. • May have unique I/T standards in each unit.
Federated Model	Autonomous business units Single company image and service model Entity follows corporate standards Corporate consolidates financials Could share some services like human resources, purchasing, and information technology	• Primarily stand-alone I/T functions but follows a consistent set of company standards. • Could be sharing common I/T infrastructure like networks, purchasing and HR systems. • Business systems and databases may run in a common data center, but they are managed independently. • Each unit may have its own external facing Website. • Major business functions could be outsourced, or some business systems are running locally. • Some online and real time interfaces across business entities exist, but most integration is done via batch processing.

Strategic Model	Business Characteristics	Architectural Characteristics
Line-of-Business	Independent sales and marketing functions Contribution margin (brand revenue) focused Multiple brand images, possibly no single corporate image Leverage corporate assets and common platforms Financial statements are sub-ledgers	• Independent sales and marketing systems are used. • Shared infrastructure like networks and customer service facilities are leveraged. • Common corporate systems like accounting, production, purchasing, and HR are relied upon. • Interfaces with corporate systems are batch database refresh and real-time on shared platforms.
Core Business	Cost control objectives Efficiency focused Maintain market share Maintain profitability Shared business functions, processes, and corporate assets	• Integrated I/T systems are the norm. • Integrated marketing channels are used to reach customers. • Corporate standards exist and are followed. • Common databases are used to support customers, suppliers and partners. • Corporate systems support the business.

Table 2—Strategy Planning Matrix

The information in table 2 can be summarized as follows:

Business Model	Enterprise Architecture Model
Holding Company	Data Interchange Architecture
Federated Model	Loosely Coupled Architecture
Line of Business	Tightly Coupled Architecture
Core Business	Integrated Architecture

Table 3—Business Architectural Models

Each enterprise architecture model represents a design pattern at the enterprise level. In the "real world," there are elements of each design pattern present in the others. There is a business model at work, which usually becomes visible in how the business has organized itself. If the predominant enterprise architecture model is mismatched with the business model, there will be many issues for the business and I/T management to contend with.

Before the enterprise system architecture can be developed to meet the needs of the enterprise, the executive teams of the business and I/T should have an understanding of the business model and which architecture model is best for the combined strategic direction. Below, each enterprise architecture model is briefly described along with a comment about the role technical standards play for each one.

The *data interchange architectural model* provides data interchange between business entities using a time-delayed store-and-forward delivery model. Specific business processes and databases within each entity are not required to function as an integrated solution and information can be delivered on a point-in-time basis. Data interchange architecture usually includes electronic data interchange (EDI) and the use of virtual private networks (VPNs) to connect businesses. The Internet can also be the delivery network connecting businesses organized as stand-alone entities assuming the appropriate security mechanisms exist. Usually, the only standards that are shared between business entities in this model are standards for data interchange. Examples of such standards are UN/EDIFACT (United Nations Electronic Data Interchange for Administration Commerce and Transport) and ebXML authored by OASIS (Organization for the Advancement of Structured Information Standards).

The *loosely coupled architectural model* is characterized by some sharing of business processes between business entities, but most information is still sent using a store-and-forward delivery model. In this case, there may be a private network which supports real-time access to systems owned and operated by the corporate function. Examples of these are general ledger and purchasing. However, since each major entity within the company functions autonomously from the core, many systems and business processes are run locally. For example, a department may have its own version of a sales database running at its facility.

The line-of-business in this case is the caretaker of its own information. Usually, a combination of private high-speed networks and loosely connected technology leveraging store-and-forward data movement are used to synchronize information across the enterprise. For example, a local system like IBM's Lotus Domino or Microsoft's Access can be used by a business unit to create a stand-alone business system. Information required to be shared with corporate entities and enterprise resource planning (ERP) systems can be moved from Lotus Domino or Microsoft Access using the file transfer protocol (FTP) in a store-and-forward data migration model. Such a design is common in a loosely coupled enterprise. Data sharing in such an environment is always a difficult problem to solve. Therefore, standards for information sharing should be established.

Loosely coupled architecture relies on data transfer standards between entities; however, I/T largely functions independently from business entity to business entity. In this model, the enterprise may either adopt one of the data transfer standards offered by independent standards bodies or utilize a semi-custom data transfer standard. If business units each have deployed ERP systems from the same vendor, then that vendor likely has a data interchange standard. For example, software marketed by SAP-AG (SAP R/3) relies on a proprietary messaging format called IDOC. To connect ERP systems from different vendors, the enterprise could utilize standards provided by the Open Applications Group (OAG) or from one of the groups proposing standards based on extensible markup language (XML).

The *tightly coupled architectural model* is characterized by extensive sharing of common databases and business processes. To share databases and business applications, information must be available in real time across a high-speed network. This architecture allows business units to "have their cake and eat it too" by supporting localized departmental systems and databases while also providing access to centralized systems like purchasing, production scheduling, and human resources over a private network in real time. In this case, the department must follow the standards set by the company's corporate I/T group. Access to such systems is provided by the company's network group, and security rules must be strictly followed; otherwise, access will be denied.

The *integrated architectural model* is characterized by total sharing of both databases and business processes (systems and programs) across the entire enterprise. Many companies have invested in ERP software to move to an integrated architecture. This architecture is intended to support lower operating costs and highly integrated processes and databases.

This model works best in a single company or entity with a common set of customers and suppliers. Most systems run in real time with some off-line batch processing to move data between the enterprise and any entity outside the core enterprise. Large companies with a global footprint may run independent operating units with stand alone systems that share data on a periodic basis. However, advancements in ERP software coupled with lower cost, higher bandwidth networks are causing system architects to consider converging disparate systems on to a single system "instance" connected by a redundant high-speed network.

Architecture Principles

We have looked at business strategy and how it relates to the four basic architecture constructs. Let's assume the business model is aligned with one of the enterprise architecture models. How can management maintain the alignment? How can a business organized into discrete lines of businesses or a federation of operating units, collaborate effectively to serve its customers and suppliers? How can senior management reduce the need for redundant systems and the costs associated with redundancy?

Just like our founding fathers struggled with a federation of colonies in 1776, senior management struggles with its disparate organization units. Our founding fathers solved the problem by drafting and gaining agreement for the Constitution of the United States of America. The constitution is a set of rules based on the principles of freedom, home rule, and representation in a government formed by the people. Enterprises also need a set of basic rules under which each "state" can operate. In the accounting profession, such rules have been long established and agreed upon. They are the rules set up by the FASB (Financial Accounting Standards Board). All businesses must follow these rules and are regularly audited by independent auditors, or they face serious legal consequences. So what would a constitution for the I/T function of a modern enterprise look like?

Architecture principles make up the constitution of the enterprise. They are not necessarily about technology but about business policy in a technical context. Architecture principles combine to form the constitution for guiding the decision making process regarding technology across the enterprise. In the process of determining the merits of a particular technology component, architecture principles will assist business managers and I/T managers, in making the right technology decisions.

Principles differ from company to company and to be most useful, principles should be managed by a governance body. The most important architecture related governance body is the

Architecture Review Board (ARB). Chapter 3 will describe the ARB and related governance bodies and procedures in detail. Many of the sample principles listed next refer to the ARB. For now however, developing a good understanding of the rule set is necessary. The following principles improve the process of maintaining synchronization between business and I/T strategic plans. They are provided in the spirit of offering good examples. Each company should develop a set of their own, based on the culture and goals of each unique business.

Centralization Principle

The enterprise-wide architecture is set by a centralized authority in the company.

The responsibility for establishing the processes and forum for planning and management of enterprise-wide architecture will be a centralized function. The central team has the ability to delegate responsibilities but retains authority and accountability for systems design integrity at the enterprise level.

Implications:

- There will be one, and only one, process in the company for setting company-wide I/T principles and standards.

Portfolio Principle

Each business system is considered to be part of an "ecosystem" of applications.

Each business system (application) is considered to be part of an "ecosystem" of applications. Applications that work together to support a particular line of business or major intersection point of business processes for the enterprise are considered part of an application portfolio. Application portfolios will line up with major sectors of the business such as *customer service* or *supplier management*. Applications within a portfolio are expected to meet a basic set of criteria established by the line of business; otherwise, they could be considered "interim" or "un-supported" applications.

Interim applications could be implemented with standards exceptions and may not be candidates for reliance on the enterprise-wide architecture principles. Interim applications expected to have a very short useful life are like scaffolding for strategic applications.

Whether an application should be considered part of the line of business portfolio of supported systems is based on how important the system is to business operations. The more users on the system or the more customers, suppliers, and financial institutions are dependent on the system, the more likely it is that it should meet enterprise standards.

Implications:

- The ARB may request that applications become fully supported, meeting company approved standards, security policies, and contingency requirements before being allowed into production.

- Applications judged to be interim or "quick hit" solutions may not be supported by I/T operations management.

- Functional teams have a responsibility to know how their application fits into the bigger picture (portfolio) of applications within their area.

Knowledge Management Principle

Data is a corporate asset.

Business systems are expected to create and maintain data, leverage information, and provide for derivation of knowledge. Data is a corporate asset and, therefore, must be inventoried, valued, protected, stored, and recoverable. All data is assigned one owner in the business community, with the authority to delegate the authority to create, read, update, and delete data. Sharing data and information with any entity external to the enterprise requires the approval of the data owner and must not conflict with company privacy policies. A ledger will be maintained for all data and information approved for sharing outside the enterprise.

Implications:

- Business owners for major data entities must be identified.
- A repository must be created to store ownership rights and what rights have been delegated by the line of business across the enterprise.
- A written external data sharing policy must exist and be published.
- A ledger must exist identifying what external companies are receiving data files from the company.

Evolutionary Principle

Business systems are expected to evolve to full functionality.

Business systems will be developed according to an approved "technology plan." Multiple plans will be maintained, each targeted at a major line of business (i.e., sales, supply chain, international, etc.). Each plan will be devised according to an evolutionary process unless there is a major business event that disrupts the evolution, such as acquisition or divestiture of a line of business. Intersections between plans will be managed through a centralized team (Project Office). The Project Office and ARB have the authority and responsibility to arbitrate issues that have a material impact across the enterprise.

Implications:

- Each major sector within the enterprise should have a plan for how systems will evolve over time to meet their business objectives.
- Plans should be presented to the ARB on a regular basis.

Design Simplicity Principle

Simplicity wins over complexity yielding best "time-to-market."

The overriding design goal of all systems is simplicity. Simplicity is the goal from a usage perspective, as well as from a maintenance perspective. Making system designs simple will yield the best possible "time-to-market," given the trade-offs of volume and functionality. The *evolutionary principle* will provide the road map to future functionality.

Implications:

- Applications are expected to utilize existing components available within the enterprise even if there is not an exact match with required functionality.
- Components are designed to be extensible to meet unknown functional requirements.
- Hiding complexity through software APIs and "wrappers" is preferable over completely rewriting callable services.

Time-to-Market Principle

Buy before build to gain time-to-market advantages.

Solutions will be purchased when possible to achieve base functionality (competitive parity). Solutions will be developed in-house when unique functionality is more important than "time-to-market," and no reasonable solution is available from outside vendors. Simplicity and "time-to-market" win over comprehensive functionality when vendor solutions exist. The *evolution* and *extensibility* principles will provide a path to full function in these cases.

Implications:

- Designers should first look within the company towards using existing components and then extend their search to the outside markets before deciding to build from scratch.

- A purchased application, component, or solution with an 80 percent functional fit is better than writing a system from scratch to achieve a 100 percent functional fit.
- Preference will be given to those vendors who have established a clear market-leading position in their industry.

Extensibility Principle

Solutions will be naturally extensible through open standards-based interfaces.

Solutions, whether purchased or developed, will be naturally extensible though open standardized interfaces. Packaged solutions supporting open, standardized, interfaces win over functionally rich systems with closed architectures.

Implications:

- All requests for information (RFI) or requests for proposal (RFP) should contain rules about what standards are required and which are optional.
- The ARB may decline a request for a purchased solution that does not provide access through APIs, callable exits, methods, or other standard interfaces.

Enablement Principle

Investments in infrastructure are necessary to enable long-term delivery consistency.

Systems will be developed according to a multilayered architectural model, with each layer being technically contained from the nonadjacent layer. Layers will provide services to other layers and will enable business functionality according to an evolutionary model. The company may make non-strategic technology investments in the short-term, which enable longer-term strategic business capability.

Implications:

- Significant infrastructure projects may be funded which have broad based business support, not necessarily from a particular line of business.
- Infrastructure projects are required to follow the company standard development methodology.

Open Standards Principle

Externally defined technology standards are used as the basis for internal standards.

Systems, and the interfaces they expose, will support standards and recommendations of an agreed upon set of external standards bodies. These include, at a minimum, the American National Standards Institute (ANSI), World Wide Web Consortium (W3C), United Nations (UN), the Open Applications Group (OAG), International Organization for Standardization (ISO), and International Telecommunications Union (ITU).

Standards across the enterprise are established by the ARB. Standards must be followed unless the ARB grants an exception in writing.

Implications:

- The ARB may deny the entry of a solution into production if it does not follow approved and documented standards.
- Vendors who follow generally acceptable standards are preferred over those who use their own homegrown standards.

Economy Principle

Technology supports business initiatives and does not stand alone.

Systems will be purchased and designed to meet the economic requirements of the *enterprise*. Meeting the economic requirements of the enterprise wins over those of a particular line of business or department. Economies are expected during all phases of system life including new development, maintenance and retirement. Systems will be designed or purchased to match the useful life of their underlying asset value, at a minimum, determined by the company's capitalization rules. Systems will be replaced on a phased basis when possible, lessening impacts on the enterprise capital plan.

Implications:

- When rendering judgment on design/implementation issues, the ARB will consider the total cost of an application. Total cost includes, design, development, implementation, conversion, run-time execution and ongoing maintenance.
- Applications that cause technical and financial stress on the network or other common services across the enterprise are required to absorb the cost of infrastructure upgrades.

Fiduciary Principle

Systems are secure and recoverable.

Systems, whether purchased or developed, will adhere to the company's approved privacy, security and disaster/recovery guidelines. All systems will be recoverable according to requirements established by the line of business, and will have the goal of minimizing disruption to customers, suppliers and trading partners of the enterprise. All systems must generate error alerts according to published error format standards. They should be included in enterprise-wide capacity planning and performance tuning initiatives.

Implications:

- All applications must meet company approved security, privacy, and contingency guidelines.

- It is a line of business responsibility to decide what level of contingency systems must meet.

- The internal audit group should be informed when an exception is granted by the ARB.

- Applications that are out of compliance must have a plan for meeting baseline policies and guidelines.

Resource Sharing Principle

All resources are company owned and shareable across line of business or department.

Resources such as software components, information, and infrastructure are shareable to minimize total cost of ownership at the enterprise level. Technology components are designed for reuse and support open standard interfaces. Business value is calculated from productivity gains associated from reuse of technology.

Implications:

- Lines of business and departments are expected to leverage existing investments in technical infrastructure.

- A repository of reusable components is required to manage common technical components.

Principle-Based Architecture

Principle-based architecture is the mechanism to gain alignment between business strategy, organization structure, and technical infrastructure. Principles form the glue that holds these three enterprise-wide pieces together over time. The difficulty is in getting agreement about the principles and then actually using them on a daily basis to manage behavior. Once agreed upon, the principles become the "invisible hand" that guides management behavior in decentralized divisions across the world. Taken together, the principles represent the constitution by which the enterprise as a whole is governed.

Drafting an initial set of principles is easy. I/T usually spearheads the first drafts of these. Done correctly, the principles stimulate discussion about business strategy and direction. For example, should the business provide private data about its customers to outside companies for a fee? This will generate a new source of revenue but at what cost to customer satisfaction? Should the business open operations in another country? If the answer is yes, then which systems should be deployed, and how should they connect with the corporate entity? To enable the discussion, I/T should generate a "straw-model" of principles and, more importantly, a set of implications for each one.

Discussion over the implications of the principles tends to make the principle based rule-set "bite" or become real. For example, a principle might say that private data about customers cannot be shared with outside companies. However, in reality, a whole department could exist, specifically set up to gain revenue from sharing data. These discussions take time and can be intense, frank, conversations about the heart of the business. It is recommended that I/T hire a professional facilitator to conduct the sessions aimed at refining the principles.

The process should start with middle managers from the business and I/T. Once basic agreement has been reached, the result-set should be shared with senior management. Expect senior management to redraft these a few times. Remember, the *process and discussion* behind generating the principles are the key benefits to the company. Once consensus has been gained, the principles can be disseminated to all operating units and utilized in a formal governance process. The governance process is described in the following chapter.

After gaining consensus on the set of principles, the new constitution can be used on a day-to-day basis by I/T and business management. The principles form a set of values which, over time, begin to permeate the minds of those tasked with making the tough calls. Should a division be allowed to buy a new database management system that no one else in the company uses, knows, or supports? If there is a principle in place that states that total cost of ownership of technology is to be minimized across the enterprise, the answer would be "no."

However, if there is a principle that says the business unit is responsible for funding any deviations from standards, then the answer could be a qualified "yes." But that business unit would need to fund the ongoing support resources, as well as the one-time project.

Summary—Chapter 2

This chapter provided management with the tools necessary to link business and I/T strategy planning. Business strategy was defined and four basic strategic organization models were presented. These were described as, *holding company model, federated model, line-of-business model,* and *core business model.* A description of how each model relates to the other was provided in a business-strategy matrix.

The I/T strategy planning process was described and a methodology to integrate I/T plans with architecture blueprints was provided. The characteristics of I/T's strategy plan were mapped to the four business model types from the business-strategy matrix, yielding four enterprise architecture models. These are the *data interchange architecture, loosely coupled architecture, tightly coupled architecture,* and the *integrated architecture.* A table for matching the correct architecture model with the corresponding business model was provided. The chapter concluded by describing how *architecture principles* maintain the synergy between strategic plans on a daily basis.

The next chapter discusses processes that manage the relationships between business strategy and I/T strategy. It reviews the need for standards and how standards help systems people do their jobs better. The chapter then focuses on the governance process and how architecture governance affects the behavior of the management team.

CHAPTER 3

Architecture Governance

So the ship has been righted, and it has found its course. However, the journey is long, and the crew is getting restless. Grumbling can be heard, and discontent is showing on their faces. Even though the captain and a few senior officers of the vessel know their destination, the crew is left in the dark. They become weary from the long trip and start to make their own plans! Avoiding mutiny is obviously a critical success factor for any ship captain. This is also very true when it comes to enterprise architecture.

There are ways in which the enterprise can govern itself. No one person has to be the focal point for managing change across the enterprise. In fact, the correct way to maintain the link between business and I/T strategy is through a systemic process. This chapter describes the need for I/T standards and defines the role they play in managing the enterprise from a technology perspective. Next, a governance process is defined. The governance process provides an ongoing systemic solution to managing I/T strategy and architecture blueprints at the enterprise level. The chapter concludes with some brief examples of how principles, standards, and a governance process can have a positive impact on management behavior across the enterprise.

I/T Standards

A common misconception in the business community is that I/T architecture equals *standards*. Standards are definitely a part of what architecture provides. However, enterprise architecture adds much more value by being the catalyst for change and by linking strategic plans across the company. The formula for providing an integrated strategic view was described in the preceding chapter. The concept of using architecture principles to link business and I/T strategy was introduced as the key to the formula. I/T standards, however, are not principles and are focused on tactics. Principles provide general guidance, where standards provide the "rules of development" for those engaged in building and maintaining technical systems across the enterprise.

Standards make it possible for I/T implementers to do their jobs faster and with confidence. Once established, standards actually become enablers to developers. Without standards, each development team would be left to invent their own "rules of development," thereby slowing down the process of building new systems.

The value of standards can be seen in the rapid growth of the Internet. The Internet was established long before it became generally popular. What really made the use of the Internet take off was an almost universal adoption of standard ways to communicate. For example, the transmission control protocol/interconnect protocol (TCP/IP) and the hypertext transfer protocol (http), along with the widespread use of the Netscape and Microsoft browser programs, made connecting to the Internet over phone lines easy and reliable.

On the server side of the Internet architecture, universal adoption of http and the hypertext markup language (html) made web pages function the same (from a technical perspective) across the world. Later, the universal adoption of the common gateway interface (CGI) made access to back-office systems possible, and the adoption of interface standards like structured query language (SQL) and open database connectivity (ODBC) enabled remote access to databases.

While it is true that most people who use the Internet don't have a clue, nor should they even care, about these standards, without them the Internet would have never taken off as fast as it did. There might have been a few pockets of collaborators on the net, but today's reach to millions of people across the world, either would have not exist or would have certainly taken much longer to achieve.

The Internet standards in place today were created by just a few technologists, and there was no one legislating these standards across the world. Although the World Wide Web Consortium (W3C) was formed to establish and certify standards, there is nothing stopping anyone or any company from building their own way to connect to the web. Behavior is controlled by voluntary compliance with the standards, as published by the W3C and other standards bodies. If someone chooses not to comply, they risk being out on an island with no one else there to communicate with.

This book does not list all the standards bodies or which technical standards exist. There are numerous web sites available which do that well. In fact, the web is the better medium for documenting dynamic content like technology standards. However, the message about using I/T standards to promote business flexibility won't change and is the focus of this chapter. I/T standards alone are not enough to deliver improved productivity and business flexibility. There must be a process in place to adjudicate adherence, motivate people to adopt, and continually challenge I/T standards.

Architecture Governance Process

The process of managing systems architecture across the enterprise is called *architectural governance*. Architecture consists of the applications, information resources, technical infrastructure and operations teams that support the business. Management of these company assets is a large responsibility that requires a high degree of collaboration across the I/T organization.

The methodology to manage technical architecture as applied to the business is composed of three major steps:

1. Develop and maintain the "constitution" in the form of principles.
2. Establish and run the "legislative branch" which sets policy, establishes technical direction, and ratifies standards.
3. Create and run the "governing body" which manages compliance and recommends changes to policy and standards.

The legislative branch in this case, is composed of the I/T leadership team. The primary entity within the legislation process is the *architecture steering committee*. The architecture steering committee meets on a monthly, quarterly, or as-needed basis. Their role is to set policy regarding technology direction for the enterprise. They rule on policy change requests, principle interpretation, and enterprise standard changes. They also issue directives to the governing body (described later) when necessary. The figure below shows committee membership and major functions performed by committee members.

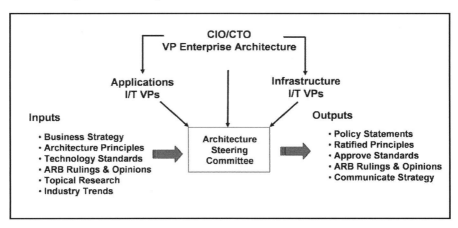

Figure 6—Architecture Steering Committee

This figure shows committee representation from the I/T function within the enterprise. Adding business planners or leadership from the business community is certainly a viable option. However, in some companies the primary job of the CIO is to interpret and represent business strategy. If business leaders can afford the time and have a genuine interest in setting I/T related policy and principles, then they should definitely be represented. In this sample model, the CIO/VP of Architecture must present requests for policy changes that affect the business to the business leadership team. Conversely, if the business sets policy or wants to change a principle, the CIO/VP of Architecture must represent these requests to the architecture steering committee.

The governing body is composed of people with technical talent from various disciplines across the enterprise. As was briefly introduced in the previous chapter, this group is called the architecture review board (ARB). To cover all aspects of technical architecture, representation is required from I/T operations, enterprise architecture, and applications/functional areas. The following figure shows what each representative area is responsible for and how they relate to the architecture steering committee and internal audit functions of the company.

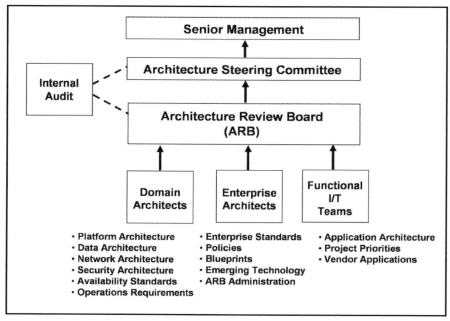

Figure 7—Governance Model

As described in chapter 2, the ARB takes into consideration the guiding principles while making decisions that impact the technical architecture of the company. Decisions are made within the context of business and I/T strategic plans. The ARB passes judgment on which standards are adopted and which standards are relaxed on a case-by-case basis. Technology industry trends and standards provide guidance on which technologies become standards within the enterprise. The figure below shows a more detailed view of the technical components that are considered by the ARB, as they address day-to-day technology issues.

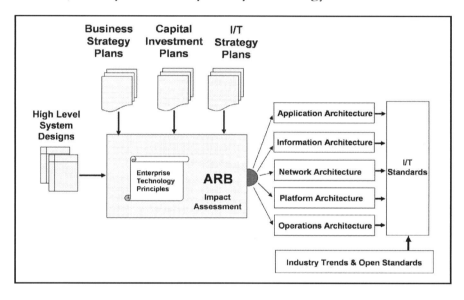

Figure 8—Architecture Review Board

The primary inputs to the ARB are high level system design documents, business strategy plans, capital plans, and I/T strategy plans. These must be understood by the review board to do the best job possible when rendering opinions about the overall technology direction of the company. Primary outputs from the board are change recommendations to the various parts of the technical architecture shown in the figure. In addition, the board is responsible for maintaining and updating the I/T standards for the company.

On a regular basis, the ARB meets to review high level systems design documents. These are reviewed to assure that company standards are met and that the application or solution presented is in agreement with the overall business and I/T strategy plans. If a proposed solution is not in agreement with the business and I/T strategic directions, the ARB has the responsibility to educate key technology leaders of the company about the proposed deviation. To demonstrate the context in which the ARB should review proposed designs, sample questions are provided for each major architectural area.

Sample Application Architecture Questions

Is this a new application or a reengineering effort for an existing application? How does this application fit in with the others within the company portfolio of applications? Does it require new approaches to communications (middleware)? Does it utilize existing middleware connectors? Are there major changes required to the company databases, files, and other information assets? Does it utilize the company approved data access programs and tools?

Sample Information Architecture Questions

What major information resources are utilized in the solution? Have provisions been made to back up and restore data? Is there a need to store data locally? If data is to be synchronized with other sources, what are the timing requirements, and what happens if data is not synchronized? Does the solution create new types of data, and is the new data useful across the enterprise? Can changes in the data for this solution affect other business processes and systems across the company? Have data entities shared with other business processes external to the solution in question been defined according to company standards?

Sample Network Architecture Questions

Does the project in question place any new requirements on the company messaging systems? Have response time targets been set, and what are the message lengths and frequencies? Does the solution require access to the Internet? Does the solution require access to services located across the network? Does the solution require access to the company information warehouses? Does the solution require connectivity with trading partners outside of the network? Have security and privacy policies and standards been addressed in the requirements and solution design?

Sample Platform Architecture Questions

Does the solution utilize the existing data center(s) and network(s) of the company? Are there any special requirements for the existing servers, mainframes, telephony systems, and networks? Is new hardware required? Does the solution utilize the standard error and event handling components of the company? What impact will the new application have on current server, disk, and network capacity? Have all groups affected by the new implementation been informed and do they agree with planned rollout schedules?

Sample Operations Architecture Questions

Has the change calendar been updated for the new system? What provisions have been made for backup and recovery? Are there service levels for the new system? What expectations does the business have regarding time to recover from unplanned outages? Are there any special maintenance requirements? Does the system run across time zones? Has the capacity plan been updated? What impacts might this system have on others running across the company?

Industry Trends and Open Standards Questions

Does the solution require any new software or hardware that is either nonstandard to the enterprise or across the technology community in general? Should the new software, hardware, or procedure be adopted as a standard within the company? Should an existing company standard be modified or amended? Should an existing company standard be dropped? Should an exception be granted in this case? What are the rules if an exception is granted, and which groups in the company will be affected?

The Virtual Chief Technology Officer

By asking questions such as these samples, the ARB can effectively act as the chief technology officer (CTO) of the company. If the company has a CTO, he or she should be the chairperson of the board. To reach maximum effectiveness, the ARB must do the following:

- Understand where the business is heading, and relate business plans to the technical direction the ARB is responsible for setting.
- "Commission" the development of high level technology plans for each of the major architectural layers as described later in chapter 4.
- Comment on the overall fit of proposed projects to the technical direction.
- Assure that all aspects of architecture have been addressed including enterprise wide security/privacy policies, and application contingency planning.
- Be ready to report gaps to senior management and respond to requests from the internal audit department.

The ARB, working with the architecture steering committee, provides the process by which architecture principles and I/T standards become part of the systems development process across the enterprise. The two groups form the legislative and governance bodies within the company and affect the behavior of the company management team. Used in conjunction with external standards bodies like ISO and others, I/T can be a semi-regulated organization within a larger sphere of organizations, much like the accountancy profession has become through FASB.

Governance and Managerial Behavior

The governance process, as defined by the architecture steering committee and the ARB, is intended to affect the behavior of I/T management on a day-to-day basis. The architecture steering committee does not set standards or dictate technical direction. Its role is to relay business strategy to the technologists of the company through the ARB. Occasionally, the committee will have to make decisions on conflicting priorities and ratify requests for new standards. However, its charter is to assure that major technical direction matches business direction in a timely and cost effective manner.

The architecture steering committee might have to decide between projects that compete for scarce resources, or decide about major investment decisions like building or buying new software applications, or whether to outsource a significant I/T function. Due to the nature of the decisions made by the architecture steering committee, it is composed of a few key I/T and business leaders.

In contrast, due to the number and complexity of technologies used within the company, the ARB is composed of a broad array of individuals. Representation should come from all the various disciplines in I/T, including data network, voice systems, database, infrastructure software, hardware, operations support and applications development. Each I/T vice president or director area responsible for a group of major business applications should have at least one person representing their area on the board.

Through equal representation on the ARB, the I/T leadership teams have a say in what standards are agreed upon and what technology solutions will be deployed within the enterprise. These are the technical experts and the most respected I/T leaders of the company. Collectively, they possess the knowledge of what has been done in the past and what new technical directions make sense to pursue in the future.

The ARB is most valuable to the enterprise when it has collective knowledge about where the business is heading, and each business functional area has presented its road-map for new development. Armed with this knowledge, the board can ratify system designs with confidence and issue change requests or even stop the purchase of software/hardware that does not fit with the companies' strategic direction. I/T management will "buy-in" to the centralized governance process if their areas are represented, and they believe that their involvement will benefit them as well as the company as a whole.

The goal of the ARB is to see that business and technology strategies are reflected in the daily decisions made by I/T management. In effect, the ARB is managing the behavior of the technology organization via its involvement in the decision-making process where the "rubber meets the road."

The ARB should maintain measurements of how many designs are reviewed and how many times adverse opinions are sent back to areas submitting design proposals. The group should publish changes to the architecture principles and I/T standards. They should also become involved in major decisions about application development tools and techniques.

They have a fiduciary responsibility to assure that systems designs adhere to company approved security, privacy, and disaster/recovery guidelines. Any system designs judged to be out of compliance should be corrected by the submitting organization, otherwise if necessary, reported to the internal audit department within the company. Typically, a more positive response will be obtained from a business or I/T area if they are given the opportunity to correct any issues and resubmit the project design proposal. Once all corrections are completed, the ARB can then sign-off on the design and approve the architecture.

But what happens when there is a real disagreement between the enterprise technology standards and the proposed project design? In all cases, the group requesting the deviation from standards has good intentions. There will always be a good business reason for the request. This puts the ARB in a difficult position. Having to trade off a short term tangible benefit within a business area, for a long term, usually intangible, enterprise-wide benefit is a difficult situation. In such cases, the board has three primary options.

They can turn down the request and document the reasons for rejection. They can allow the request and ask the I/T team who submitted the proposal or request when and how the deviation from standards will be brought into compliance. A third alternative would be to update the I/T standards and adopt the proposal. In any event, statistics about the request and recommended position should be documented.

Below are a few sample metrics that should be captured by the ARB. Your company may also create new or different metrics per your unique governance requirements.

- How many high level designs were reviewed over what time period?
- How many adverse opinions (rejections) were published?
- How many designs were approved?
- How many designs were approved with exceptions to company standards?
- How many designs resulted in creating new standards?
- What costs were saved by reusing existing solutions?

Capturing metrics like these is critical to managing the architecture governance process. They are used to show the value of the governance process when teams question the viability of the architecture steering committee and the ARB.

Chapter 3—Summary

This chapter described how architecture principles are used to link strategy with day-to-day decision making by I/T leaders across the company. It described the role I/T standards play in the context of *principle-based architecture*. Standards represent the tactical "rules for development," while principles embody the link between business strategy and I/T strategy.

Once principles and standards have been agreed upon across the enterprise, a process to maintain the agreement on a daily basis was described. The architecture governance process was defined as a combination of the architecture steering committee and the ARB. The two committees enable I/T management with knowledge of business strategic direction. By supporting the architectural governance processes, management is free to execute on their plans, remaining confident of meeting the strategic goals of the enterprise. The chapter concluded with brief comments about how behavior is affected by architecture principles, standards, and committees. Sample quality control metrics for the governance processes were presented.

The following chapters provide a generic architecture blueprint for the enterprise. Chapter 4 outlines the major technology components present in most business entities. It serves as an outline of a common systems architectural framework. Each major part of the framework is then defined in detail in chapters 5-9.

CHAPTER 4

Architecture Framework

By using navigational technology and communicating the strategy behind the voyage, our crew has successfully and safely found their destination. We applaud them for their endurance and congratulate them on their success. The analogy of being lost at sea, albeit simplistic, is how many I/T leaders feel regarding business and I/T strategy planning. The first three chapters provided a formula for linking business and I/T strategy. However, strategic plans aren't valuable if the enterprise is unable to follow through. A company will have difficulty executing their plans if the underlying I/T architecture lacks flexibility.

This chapter introduces the technical aspects of I/T architecture. It presents an overview of the major technology components that comprise the enterprise systems architecture of most companies. The next five chapters each define the I/T disciplines and technology that run today's companies. These technical areas have been organized into "layers" that support the overall structural integrity of the enterprise. This combination of layers is called the *enterprise architecture framework.*

So what is an enterprise architecture framework? An analogy taken from the construction industry helps to answer that question. Think of a brick building. It looks strong, doesn't it? It is strong, but not because of the brick exterior. The brick adds some strength, but what makes the building really strong is its internal frame.

Usually, there is a steel center beam surrounded by concrete pillars and steel or wood studs. The brick is put on after the inside of the building has been constructed. The framework takes the stress of the roof and keeps the walls from coming in on one another. The brick exterior is the finishing touch that makes the building look strong. It does add value by keeping wind and rain away from the inside. However, the building is only as strong as its frame.

What makes up the *framework* of systems within the enterprise? What happens if the business changes and the framework can't support it any longer? Can the business enter new markets or shut down unprofitable operations given the existing I/T framework? In the information technology industry, the term *framework* is used for a number of different things. There are software frameworks, object frameworks, database frameworks, and others. In the enterprise architecture context, a framework represents the basic technology components that make up the stable pillars of the enterprise's systems.

These include applications (software), information (files and databases), network (including voice messaging and transaction processing), platforms (hardware) and I/T operations management. The following figure generally shows the major layers of technology that comprise the enterprise architecture framework. Each technical layer works with the others to provide functionality, stability and flexibility to the business.

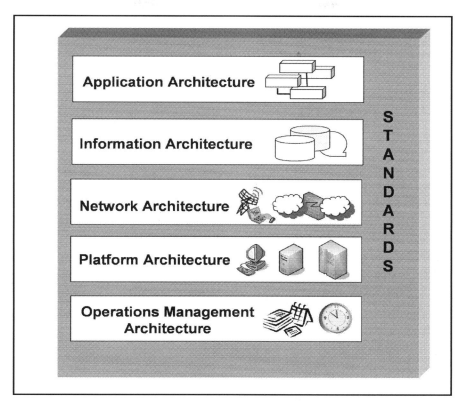

Figure 9—Enterprise Architecture Framework

Figure 9 is a conceptual view to an enterprise architecture framework. The background signifies standards that apply to all layers. For example, there are standards that apply to applications, databases, messaging, networks, and hardware platforms. The operations management layer applies to all layers above. For example, there are change control procedures that apply to hardware, networks, messaging systems, databases and application software. The hardware and system software components reside within the platform architecture layer. Networks of all types reside within the network architecture layer. Security technology is also part of this layer. Next, information architecture includes data management polices and procedures, as well as the databases and file systems of the enterprise. At the top of the architecture model is the application layer. This area is where the software architecture resides for the company. It includes the standards for developing and running the systems that run the business.

The following subsections of this chapter will briefly define each major layer of the model in figure 9. Chapters 5-9 will delve into each particular layer in more detail. Taken together, these form the base constructs of the enterprise architecture. The particular vendor technology and homegrown solutions used to carry out the functions in a particular layer may differ from company to company. However, capabilities described for each layer of the architecture form the enterprise architecture from a logical perspective.

Application Architecture

By now, most everyone is aware of applications (computer software). We all work with them every day whenever we go to an ATM or make phone call or buy something at a major retailer. Even young children are using applications on the web to build personalized web sites and download games and music. Applications have evolved greatly over the years. Anyone who has been in the I/T industry for a number of years remembers what applications were like in the 1960s and 70s. By looking at the progression of these systems over the years, we can make some educated guesses about where things are heading. The following figure shows the association between business applications and the underlying technology innovations that made them possible.

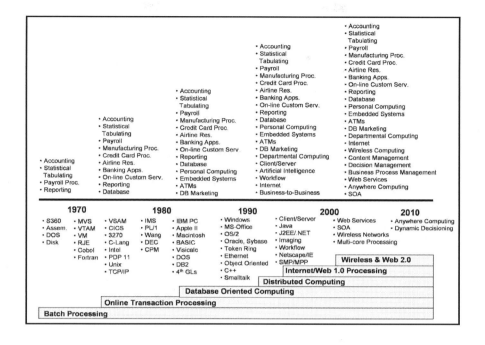

Figure 10—Application Evolution

As systems technologies improved over the years, the number and complexity of business applications has grown. This is quite obvious; however, what's not so obvious is the progression of the *type* of computing. The progression from batch processing to online transaction processing, to database oriented computing, to distributed computing, to Internet/Web 1.0, to wireless and Web 2.0, is quite logical. As the industry moved to the next level of computing, the prior levels remained intact and continued to service business users.

For example, it makes sense to run the payroll application in batch mode as it is needed by the business periodically. However, making updates to an employee's salary record should be accomplished via online screens from an authorized agent of the company. Information about human resources can be analyzed and distributed into departmental systems, and employees can access their 401K balances via voice or web browser using a secured Internet connection. As the figure shows, layering of business applications over the years has created an ever escalating problem of complexity for I/T management.

The application architecture is a composition of the newest most innovative systems together with thirty plus years of "legacy" systems. Connections between these systems were usually developed on an as-needed basis using different technologies, protocols, and standards. All this confusion has cost companies billions in inefficient business processes, redundant applications, and databases. The chapter on "Application Architecture" will discuss ways to improve the usefulness of applications while reducing support costs. It covers software frameworks, common objects, reuse, packaged software, and the application service provider (ASP) model.

Information Architecture

Information technology produces one and only one product—that is, *information*. This is an obvious statement. However, when people think of I/T, many think in terms of programs, databases, networks, and hardware. These components are organized to deliver information to people or to other systems. Why is it then that many large companies don't spend more time, effort and money on management of their information, as if it were an asset of the company?

A sign of a company's commitment to information management is the presence of an "inventory control" system for information. Is there technology in place which identifies and tracks information, as it is used across the enterprise? Has the company established management roles for controlling and monitoring information use, inside and outside the company? By answering these questions, one can determine if a company has matured regarding treating information as a company asset.

The chapter on "Information Architecture" defines what is necessary to manage information at the enterprise level, as an asset of the firm. The chapter also cites why investments in information management resources deliver lasting value to the business. It provides a model for categorizing information, making it easier to manage in a cost effective manner. The chapter concludes with a description of an information architecture showing how data used to run business operations relates to data used in new product development.

Network Architecture

If information is I/T's product, the *network* is the delivery channel. The evolution in network technology has been as dramatic as the application evolution over the last thirty years. Wide area networks (WANs) grew from the extensive analog voice infrastructure developed by long distance providers, as well as the "bell operators" in local markets. Local area networks (LANs) grew from the need to link PCs and share file servers and printers in offices.

Today, connectivity between LANs, WANs, and the Internet are critical elements in any enterprise-wide architecture. Since application performance can be no faster than the slowest part of any network, finding the optimum network architecture is a critical success factor of all businesses. Chapter 7, covering "Network Architecture", explores how networks contribute to the growth and success of the business, regardless of primary industry. The chapter also describes the emergence and growth of cellular and other wireless networks. It discusses how various forms of wireless network technologies can be used in new and innovative ways, driving business growth.

A brief introduction to payment networks is provided and a model for integrating payment networks, the Internet and cellular networks is presented. The chapter concludes with a high level description of security architecture and a model for integrating various security solutions is presented.

Platform Architecture

Platforms are what most people think of when they think of computer systems. Platforms are composed of hardware and software that defines the foundation of the enterprise from a systems perspective. Platforms include mainframes, file servers, web servers, application servers, disk storage systems, tape management systems, PCs and the software that makes them run. (Networks also have platforms such as firewalls, switches and routers, but these are not the focus of this chapter).

For many businesses, the pace of computing is defined by the size and speed of its networks and primary platforms. For example, a financial institution such as a bank can only run as fast as its core batch processes. The core processes dictate the "processing day" because account balances must be updated to reflect new activity before being turned over to the customer service, lending and collections departments. Some companies have moved beyond the constraints of batch processing "windows" and run transaction processing systems all day. Even these must deal with "maintenance windows" and must stop their online systems or run off a backup set of systems during maintenance periods.

The chapter on "Platform Architecture" discusses the key topics regarding hardware that apply to the enterprise. Topics such as platform selection, scalability, virtualization, and storage architecture are covered. A methodology for selecting the correct platform for the computing job is provided. A model for determining whether to "scale-up" or "scale-out" is provided. The chapter closes with a discussion of how computer operating system virtualization can help reduce processing costs at the enterprise level.

Operations Management Architecture

If the enterprise cannot maintain high availability and response time stability, or is unable to manage error conditions effectively, it will not be able to use technology strategically. There are times when the business gets frustrated with I/T even in the best-run companies, but serious systems issues must be rare (or at least be hidden from customers, suppliers, and business users). The chapter on "Operations Management Architecture" addresses these issues.

Operations management is part of the overall enterprise architecture framework. It is defined as those processes, procedures and standards that "keep the I/T lights on". This chapter provides a description of the major functions associated with I/T operations management. These include problem management, change management, configuration management, asset management and capacity planning. An architecture model linking these is described. The concept of the enterprise architecture repository is introduced and a description of how it can be used by I/T operations is presented.

Chapter 4—Summary

This chapter marked the beginning of a technology focus. It opened by defining a high level enterprise architecture framework. The framework contains each of the major architectural layers present at the enterprise level regardless of company or industry. The entire framework is backed by various standards that exist within each technical layer.

The layers of the enterprise architecture framework include applications architecture, information architecture, network architecture, platform architecture, and operations management architecture. An introduction to each of these topics was provided including examples of why they are important to the overall enterprise architecture framework.

The following chapter describes how applications established at the enterprise level, meet the overriding mission of the business while still providing for flexibility and cost-effectiveness.

Chapter 5

Application Architecture

Applications run the business processes that deliver value to shareholders. The software programs that run the enterprise define the character of the enterprise as much as the brand image or advertising program. Consumers expect to walk into a store of a major retailer and be serviced quickly and without error at the checkout counter. Poorly performing applications will cause frustration on the part of the consumer as well as the store employee. In a negative scenario like this, no one ends up happy, and the business suffers from lost market share to a better-performing competitor.

In some cases, the manner in which applications perform is a matter of life or death. In health care, systems that run within a hospital must be easy to use by a complex patchwork of professionals. Information has to be timely and accurate; otherwise, patients could receive the wrong dosages of medicine or even be treated for erroneous symptoms.

Applications Run Industries

Companies have struggled over the years building, buying, installing, and running large complex applications. It is interesting to note that some of the most successful applications running today (measured by how long they were used and their level of importance to operations) were originally based on what many would consider to be old technology. For example, the base system running the two most successful airline reservation systems (APOLLO for Galileo, a division of UAL, and SABRE for AMR) were designed in the 1970s. These systems were created on an architectural base called TPF (transaction processing facility). TPF is an operating system developed by IBM to answer the specific needs of industries with high online transaction volumes that must be supported on a seven-day by twenty-four-hour by 365 days/ year basis. How was TPF designed to meet the needs of an entire industry and remain vital for over thirty years? TPF was designed to perform a discreet set of functions at high speed with little or no downtime. Two basic architectural constructs set the design tone for the entire system and eventually set the operating pace of an entire industry. These basic design constructs are *a common record size* for data and a *transaction queuing system.*

To meet business requirements of subsecond transaction response time and high availability, TPF relies on a few standard data record sizes. Data files consist of small standardized records that are indexed by a TPF data access indexing system. Being of standard size, records are managed by disk storage devices and can be stored (cached) in machine memory, yielding the fastest information retrieval times possible. Any data can be stored and delivered to an online program, as long as it meets the standard format structure for TPF. Record sizes are limited to 256 bytes, 512 bytes, or 1,024 bytes. There is a standard "header" for each record and a data "payload" area. By constraining all records to this format, the system designers were assured that data would be easily accessed and could fit into any network architecture.

A transaction-queuing system handles inbound and outbound transactions from the centralized mainframes that run TPF. Since the information is stored using standard record sizes, response times and throughput improve, as hardware and network technology improves without reorganizing or restructuring the TPF file system.

To reach the high availability goal, there are redundant TPF systems in multiple physical locations. Leveraging the transaction queuing system and discrete record sizes, updates to files are quickly replicated across a network to backup systems. To provide the highest availability, there are three complete systems running at all times. There is enough capacity to run the entire transaction volume on two of the three systems with an undetectable degradation in response time. Therefore, maintenance can be performed to one of the systems while the others are up and running. Systems can be switched in round-robin style allowing the installation of software changes without impacting online availability.

Other applications that added value, such as seat pricing, yield management, flight scheduling, crew scheduling, ticketing, and billing were added to the architecture as time progressed. These and other systems run outside of the base environment and are even called *offline* systems by I/T personnel within the airline industry. The so called, offline systems, all have online transaction capabilities and most use relational databases within their core architecture. However, they run on their own schedules and deliver updates to the *online* world of TPF on a periodic basis.

This application architecture caused some interesting things to occur from a competitive business perspective. For example, one of the most important ways airlines compete is through their ability to change prices quickly. This is called "yield management" within the airline industry. Changing seat prices is a very complicated business process. There are thousands of flights per day scheduled by every airline. Each seat on each flight is priced according to a complex set of parameters such as the date the seat was purchased, location within the aircraft, and air mileage between the origin and destination cities.

So when an airline wants to change pricing in certain flight segments, they run an intricate set of business rules that calculate the yield, or net return, on the seats in a market for a specific time period. When one airline publishes new fares or discount programs, competitors must respond as quickly as they can. It becomes a competition of which I/T team can deliver pricing changes from their yield management system to their TPF environment the fastest. A few years ago, it would take up to three days to change a large number of fares. Now the timeframe has been reduced to one day or less and most airlines are at parity when it comes to "price wars" from a systems perspective.

The consumer credit card industry has also been defined by its applications architecture. In the 1960s, a credit card processing application was developed to process large volumes of credit card transactions. Since the predominant technology at the time was the IBM 360 Mainframe running the disk operating system (DOS), processing was all batch oriented. Disk technology was very expensive then, so magnetic tape was the fastest and most cost-effective means to process large volumes of transactions against large numbers of credit card accounts.

Processing update transactions sequentially requires sorting the input transactions in low to high order. The input file of update transactions is called a "batch." Once the input has been sorted in ascending sequence, it can be matched with the ascending sequenced target file to be updated called the "master file." In the 1960s and early 1970s this type of processing ran the fastest because mainframes and storage devices were designed to process information most efficiently when it was organized sequentially and run in large batches.

In the early 1970s, IBM developed the Multi-Virtual Operating System (MVS) and the Virtual Telecommunications Access Method (VTAM). Then in the mid 1970s, the Customer Information Control System (CICS) was offered by IBM to support online transaction processing from terminals. MVS/VTAM and CICS work together to this day providing companies with support for high volume, low response time, online transaction processing using a mainframe computer.

During the time IBM was making advances in mainframe computing, a company called First Data Resources (FDR) developed credit card processing systems for banks that issued credit cards. Taking advantage of the new software made available by IBM in the 1960s and 1970s, FDR developed what would become the core set of applications that drove the credit card industry for decades.

Because FDR's core application architecture was based on a batch-processing model, systems ran updates to the master file at very high speed. This architecture met the needs of banks with millions of credit card accounts for applying updates and generating credit card statements.

As IBM developed online systems, customer service applications were added by FDR, to the batch oriented card processing architecture. Most banks that issued credit cards collected updates in online files during daily operations and applied the updates to the master file in batch jobs scheduled to run when the bank's branches were closed. The time between when last update was captured in the online files and when the batch master file was finished being updated, was called the "batch window." The information in the master file did not match the information in the online files until the entire overnight update process was completed and the online files were refreshed with new data.

For many banks, the update and refresh process established in the 1970s remains in effect even today. If there is too much input volume or there are problems running the batch process to completion, the online files cannot be refreshed with the most current information in time for the next business day to begin. Therefore, the challenge was, and still is in many cases, keeping the "batch window" from impacting the online processing day.

From an industry perspective, the batch processing architectural model took hold and became the de facto standard for processing credit card transactions. Then in the 1990s, major credit card issuers and processors began using relational databases to process transactions. Database technology reduced the time information would be out of date by extending the online capabilities of these systems and reducing the batch-window. However, in most cases, there are still batch oriented processes like credit card statement processing that require a batch processing window.

These examples taken from the airline industry and the credit card industry show how application architecture can affect not only how a business operates, but in some cases, how entire industries operate. The remainder of this chapter describes how application architectures are maturing given the new architectural models of N-tier software, enterprise resource planning, application service providers, and wireless computing.

Evolving Application Architecture

Software design has evolved dramatically over the years. However, as we have seen for applications designed years ago, when a new approach is added, the older approaches continue to be useful. Therefore, the enterprise of today is faced with maintaining "legacy" software that was designed in the last four decades, as well as adopting the newest software development techniques. Just as the airline and consumer credit and banking industries leveraged common software designs, today we have software *frameworks*.

A software framework is a combination of standards, communication protocols, interface specifications, and programming guidelines. Today, the newest software programming models, or frameworks, revolve around Java Enterprise Edition, the Microsoft .NET (pronounced "dot net") Framework, and Web-services. What are these, and how do they work with the great designs of the past? Most importantly, how do frameworks add value to the enterprise, and why are they important to the business?

There are many frameworks available for all kinds of software development. The most well-known frameworks originate from IBM, Sun Microsystems, BEA Systems, Microsoft, and various "open source" work groups. Two well-known "open source" work groups are the Jakarta Project (*www.jakarta.apache.org*) that provides software frameworks aimed at the Java programming language and the Java Enterprise Edition software model; and the code project (*www.codeproject.com*) which promotes sharing solutions developed with the Microsoft .NET Framework.

Software frameworks made available through companies like IBM, Sun Microsystems, BEA Systems, and Microsoft have their origins in the open standards groups. For example, the W3C (World Wide Web Consortium, *www.w3.org*) is the author of various standards. The W3C develops reviews and approves standards for inclusion in published specifications. The specifications are then used as input to the creation of software frameworks by vendors and independent software developers and engineers. Some frameworks are free and others require license fees. Teams of developers collaborating over the Internet create additional components and make these available for free on web sites.

The industry leading software companies pay close attention to making their frameworks compliant with published open standard recommendations. They actively participate in and drive open standards research and development. Examples of organizations committed to developing open standards include OASIS (the Organization for the Advancement of Structured Information Standards, *www.oasis-open.org*), the W3C, UDDI (Universal Description Discovery and Integration, *www.uddi.org*), the OMG (Object Management Group, *www.omg.org*), and UN/CEFACT (United Nations Centre for Trade Facilitation and Electronic Business, *www.uncefact.org*). This is only a sampling of organizations devoted to the advancement of software architecture, but these are among the most influential.

The software architectures of the past were defined by the underlying technology available at the time. A sequential processing model in batch mode was the "framework" for software architecture beginning in the 1960s. Online systems were defined by CICS in the 1970s. IMS (information management system) introduced the database framework in the early 1980s, and in the 1990s, relational databases combined with distributed processing, defined how applications were designed. There are three major "frameworks" driving the application architecture of today and into the future. These are the N-Tier Software Framework, Web-services, and Wireless Data Access. Each of these models represents a significant driving factor shaping not only the I/T industry but also the way business will be done over the coming years.

N-Tier Software Framework

The N-Tier Software Framework is based on each layer of the application architecture being optimized to do a particular job. Each layer is able to communicate with its adjacent layer through standard interface protocols. The figure below is a logical representation of this design.

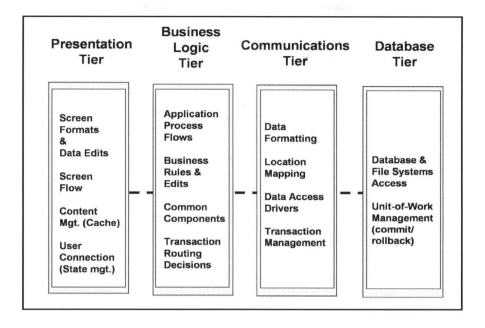

Figure 11—N-Tier Software Framework

This framework separates program logic, designed for presentation of content on the screen, from business logic that performs calculations and edits, from network communications components and data access programs.

Through this separation, applications become modular, scalable, and accessible over a network. Additionally, performance of each layer can be optimized through the use of hardware and software services specially designed for the functions performed at that particular layer. For example, web server software can be assigned to a machine that just supports the presentation tier. Application server software can be applied to the business logic tier. Communications software can be assigned to a dedicated server in the communications tier. Hardware and software can be assigned to optimize processing in the database tier.

If software is designed according to this architectural framework, a company has the flexibility to connect business programs (logic) to databases that reside in other parts of the world. Since business logic is separated from the way the information is presented, data can be reused and accessed from systems that are external to the immediate environment. A business that adopts this framework has positioned itself to experience the following major benefits:

- improve time-to-market for new applications
- reduce ongoing software maintenance costs
- leverage existing investments in software and databases
- open and secured access to strategic business processes for customers and suppliers
- isolation of changes to software and hardware in specific tiers or layers

The N-Tier Software Framework has tremendous implications for business. Getting the same answer to a question no matter from where in the world the question is asked, or which type of device is used to do the asking, can break down the barriers of space and time. Anything that can be digitized can be delivered in real time to anyone authorized, anywhere.

While the N-Tier Software Framework is a concept, a few technology companies have developed products to put it into practical use. Companies such as IBM, Microsoft, Sun Microsystems, BEA Systems, and others have developed solutions to help I/T deliver the value associated with the N-Tier Software Framework. These software vendors follow the design specifications of OASIS, OMG, and the W3C. There is some divergence between those supporting the Java 2 Platform Enterprise Edition (J2EE) specification and those supporting Microsoft's .NET Framework. (Microsoft supports Java, but not the entire J2EE specification).

Microsoft's .NET Framework was developed, to a certain degree, independently from the J2EE effort. However, all significant vendors are backing the Web-services specifications. These specifications are based on the Web-services Definition Language (WSDL) and the Simple Object Access Protocol (SOAP)

XML specifications. Both of these specifications are supported by the W3C.

The Java 2 Platform Enterprise Edition (J2EE) framework is an important specification from Sun Microsystems for implementing the N-Tier architecture. The software framework has been written about in numerous books, magazines, and "white papers." The reader is encouraged to seek other references for detailed descriptions of the J2EE specifications. Since J2EE is a *specification* and not a software product from a company, any company is free to create an implementation of the specification.

All products developed from the specifications support the Enterprise Java Bean (EJB) specification. Enterprise Java Beans are programs written in the Java language that conform to an interface standard. The interface standard makes "beans" callable and reusable regardless of their underlying run time platform. Software vendors supporting the J2EE and EJB programming specifications have developed software that optimizes their particular interpretation of the specification. Utility level software programs that support J2EE called "application servers" have implementation differences across vendor solutions.

From an enterprise architecture perspective, there isn't enough functional difference between the vendor provided J2EE compliant products to significantly impact business operations. The important architectural consideration is adopting the N-Tier model and the standards it provides across the enterprise.

The framework offered by Microsoft to build applications that match the N-Tier architecture model is called .NET. Microsoft's .NET architecture is based on the concept of "web enabling" current and existing technologies. Web enabling, in this context, means making components accessible using a standard interface specification, defined in XML using the Simple Object Access Protocol (SOAP).

The .NET architecture includes the underlying Microsoft operating systems, Microsoft Enterprise Servers, prepackaged XML Web-services called .NET My Services, Microsoft Visual Studio, and a developer's platform called the .NET Framework. The technology used by I/T to build applications meeting the N-Tier architecture model from Microsoft is the .NET Framework.

While .NET is not a specification like J2EE from a consortium of companies, Microsoft is a leader in driving the Web-services and SOAP specifications in the W3C. The .NET Framework depends heavily on these two open specifications. The .NET Framework supports a library of *types*. Types are software components that are comparable to EJBs. Types can be programs written in a variety of programming languages. By supporting the Web-services and SOAP specifications, types can become callable routines that exhibit behavior similar to that of EJBs.

For companies with an investment in software developed with Microsoft's programming tools, the .NET Framework provides considerable value. Non-Microsoft programs are able to coexist with Microsoft developed software on the same server architecture. Using the .NET Framework and open integration standards, software architects in a predominantly Microsoft oriented software shop, can build N-Tier solutions spanning both J2EE and .Net frameworks.

What's important about either J2EE or .NET from a business perspective, is how they improve time-to-market, reduce software maintenance costs, and support customers and suppliers. It is the job of the enterprise architecture team to make the business case for the N-Tier Software Framework. The team should evaluate the costs and benefits of adopting the N-Tier architecture model and select the best delivery platform for the enterprise.

Web-services and the N-Tier Software Framework

Web-services, as defined by the W3C, are aimed at making business logic reusable from systems that are outside of a contained environment. A business process like a *mortgage interest rate calculator* can be defined using the web-services definition language (WSDL), making it an executable module to any other system that also supports WSDL. By combining WSDL with the extensible markup language (XML), any program can then gain access to the *mortgage interest rate calculator* across a network and get the same results as any other calling program. This is a powerful concept that helps an enterprise not only solve issues of data redundancy and improved accuracy but allows the enterprise to share business processes with customers, suppliers, and partners across the Internet or a private network.

By combining Web-services with the N-Tier Software Framework, business logic becomes accessible via XML messages across a network. By moving the business logic of the application to the server side of the network, the desktop computer need not be as function rich. This means that the same business function can be run from an attached PC or non-PC such as a cellular phone or personal digital assistant (PDA). The Web-services specification contains a description of the simple object access protocol (SOAP). A program written to process SOAP messages can interoperate over any network (internal or the Internet) with a business function defined as a web service. Additional information about Web-services can be found in chapter 10, Service-Oriented Architecture, and on the W3C Web site, *www.w3c.org/ws/*.

Wireless Access and the N-Tier Software Framework

The *Wireless Access Framework* is based on standard messaging architectures that support digital data transmissions between mobile devices and company back-office systems. The framework is based on a network transport layer composed of the global system for mobile communications (GSM), the general packet radio service (GPRS), and wideband code division multiple access (WCDMA). These three technologies provide wireless access to the Internet from cell phones and other wireless devices.

While GSM/GPRS/WCDMA provides digital voice and data transportation services, the message content is packaged in the wireless access protocol (WAP). WAP is sponsored by a consortium of businesses known as the Open Mobile Alliance (OMA). Since its inception, the WAP standard was adopted by the W3C and has evolved into WAP 2.0. WAP 2.0 is a set of wireless access standards that utilize extensible hypertext markup language (xhtml) for messaging standards. GSM/GPRS/WCDMA and WAP work together to provide an open medium for delivering digital information to users over cellular networks. There are more topics to consider when enabling applications for access over cellular networks. These are explored in more detail in chapter 7, Network Architecture.

Wireless computing presents I/T with a new model for application delivery. Being always on and always connected, people can access information any time from any where in the world. The combination of digital cellular and Internet technologies breaks down barriers such as the limited radio spectrum and limited broadcast distances. Information in small "bursts" can be sent and received between individuals who are known by a unique address and computer servers anywhere in the world. For example, a customer service application that was only available within a call-center or via a PC's Internet web browser, could be accessed from anywhere in the world from a mobile device. Web-services extend the application to a WAP gateway. The WAP gateway presents a customized user interface suitable for cell phones, smart phones and personal digital assistants (PDAs).

The N-Tier Software Framework combined with the Wireless Access Framework provides business with the ability to reuse software objects (components) not only across the enterprise but also with customers, suppliers, and partners. Wireless enabled applications utilize digital cellular networks to deliver information to individuals connected to always-on computing platforms around the globe. The application architecture required to deliver this functionality is available, and an example of it is shown in the following figure.

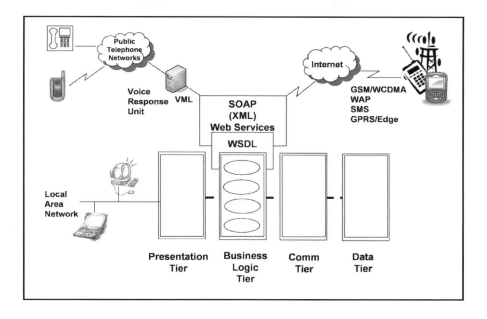

Figure 12—Wireless Access Framework

The figure shows how application logic designed for in-house use can be extended to a variety of networks and devices. The power of breaking the application into four discrete layers is apparent. Many corporations are working on this type of architecture and will continue to extend business services to customers, suppliers, and partners in the coming years. The next section describes how the N-Tier Software Framework can be extended even further.

Enterprise Resource Planning (ERP) Applications

Enterprise resource planning (ERP) applications have their roots in the data centralization theme of the 1980s. The basic concept is that business processes are optimized by using common enterprise-wide databases. This idea was manifested in the early release of SAP (R/2), which was based on a central relational database running on the mainframe. Oracle followed suit and released Oracle Enterprise Resource Planning software. Other major entrants into the ERP business were BAAN and Peoplesoft (later acquired by Oracle), JD Edwards, Lawson and others. Regardless of the particular vendor solution, from an enterprise architecture perspective, companies implement ERPs to gain the following major benefits:

- standardize and optimize business processes
- integrate business processes across organizational units
- deliver a single "source of truth" for enterprise data resources
- reduce interface proliferation
- reduce I/T support costs
- improve customer service
- improve manufacturing processes
- establish standard accounting practices
- provide better management reports
- improve inventory balances
- reduce days outstanding on receivables
- integrate supply chains
- integrate demand chains
- improve systems availability and stability

ERPs are architected to deliver these benefits to any enterprise, regardless of industry. By implementing an ERP, an enterprise inherits the design decisions made by the software package designers. All packages are based on a logical database design that delivers high integrity of information. Information integrity is achieved through a controlled set of edit rules that are consistently applied when data is put into the system. Therefore, from an enterprise perspective, an ERP can be viewed as a "black box." The black box contains valid business rules for the business functions that are enabled through the ERP software. Applications outside of the ERP's domain, such as a custom developed application, communicate with the ERP through the ERP's standard interface protocols.

Business process flexibility is governed by the ERPs ability to accommodate changes in processing rules and data flows. For example, if a company developed a stand-alone web system that contained edit criteria for orders placed over the Internet that are different than the ERP's criteria, orders could be rejected by the ERP. System errors that result from poor ERP integration delay order processing and introduce new errors, as orders are manually entered.

The complexity associated with integrating in-house developed software with ERP systems is a major design consideration. ERP software vendors as well as other companies have developed technology called enterprise application integration (EAI) software to solve this integration problem. EAI and other integration technologies are discussed in more detail in chapter 10, Service-Oriented Architecture. The following figure is an example of using EAI and Web-services to integrate in-house applications with an ERP suite.

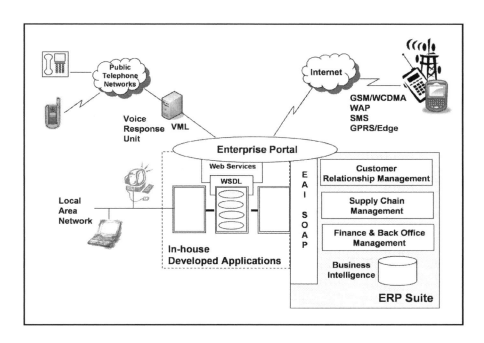

Figure 13—Application Architecture and ERPs

Figure 13 shows how an ERP is part of a larger enterprise model that includes in-house software. Custom-developed applications that have been enabled for the Internet via Web-services can be "bolted on" the front end of the ERP using EAI adapters designed for the particular ERP solution.

Quite often, companies want to manage external information flows through a common managed portal. The enterprise portal shown in the figure provides security and online access services across the enterprise. The overall integration architecture shown in figure 13 preserves the integrity of the information managed by the ERP system. The integration architecture also provides business processes that are differentiated from competitors who have implemented the same ERP software.

An architecture that includes a mixture of both in-house developed software and ERP software provides the following business benefits:

- Provides a platform to differentiate products and services for customers, partners, and suppliers.

- Provides a "back-end" that standardizes business processes across organization units and geography.

- Delivers consistent accounting practices and policies on a worldwide scale.

- Opens up information stored deep within the ERP databases through the "portal" that supports open interface standards.

- Enables centralized management of the complex technologies needed to connect in-house software with packaged software.

- Enables centralized management of integration technologies, security, and standards to extend services to business partners, customers and suppliers.

Obtaining the benefits listed above of mixing in-house and ERP software is made feasible through adoption of integration technologies as described in this chapter and in later in chapter 10.

Application Service Provider Model

The application service provider (ASP) model gained popularity during the dot-com boom in the late 1990s. Many senior managers of the largest companies in the world saw that "first mover advantage" was a critical success factor in staking out territory in the vast Internet space. Both business-to-consumer (B2C), as well as business-to-business (B2B) types of Internet business models saw value in being first to reach the market. Since many companies didn't have enough people skilled in "e-business", some companies decided to outsource their dot-com I/T infrastructure and support. To respond to the high immediate demand, new companies were formed almost over night, to provide web-hosting services. Even the largest companies like IBM, EMC[2] and AT&T, got into the web hosting business.

However, with the stock market valuation correction in 2001, many dot-com businesses lost their funding and went bankrupt. Along with the "dot bomb" of 2001 came the closing of some very large businesses focused on hosting web systems. But, as some web hosting companies went out of business, something interesting was going on from an application software perspective. The web hosting companies that remained were running some mission critical systems like ERPs and customer service systems for small and medium-sized businesses. Some of these hosting businesses became application service providers and the ASP model was born.

ASPs run packaged and custom-developed software on behalf of companies. Applications that rely on the web browser as their front-end can easily take advantage of the ASP model. These "browser-based applications" don't need to be attached to a private network to be able to utilize enterprise services. The major advantage to the enterprise of the ASP model is lower I/T operating costs. This is possible, as ASP providers spread fixed costs associated with hardware and software license fees across a broad customer base. With the ASP model, the same physical hardware is sometimes used to run applications servicing multiple client companies.

The ASP model of today is similar to what timesharing was decades ago. Timesharing was based on the premise that computing power was high cost and difficult to manage. By sharing the time (or excess capacity) on expensive mainframe computers, companies needed to pay only for the capacity they utilized on a time or transactional basis. This model worked for businesses that didn't need high degrees of customization in their software solutions and could afford to run according to the schedules set by the service provider.

How does the ASP model fit in with the application architecture of the future? As major corporations manage the risks of new startup ventures, they may decide to move the I/T function of the new venture to an outside support firm. Additionally, as more applications are designed to take advantage of the N-Tier Software Framework, there is benefit in lower operating costs resulting from paying for only the service used, rather than excess capacity. Users can gain access from internal networks, virtual private networks, and the Internet to software hosted by the ASP. ASP vendors can manage isolated hardware capacity to particular customers while leveraging the highest cost element of the ASP support model, support labor, across many customers.

The issues with the ASP model are similar to those experienced by the companies who opted for the timesharing model of the 1970s. As hardware costs continue to decline, the cost of capital makes buying or leasing equipment more attractive than the ASP model. Also, ASPs make money by leveraging as many customers as possible across the smallest fixed cost base as possible. This sets up an inherent conflict of goals between customers and suppliers for computing capacity. Customers will always be looking for faster, more powerful computing service while the incentive for the ASP is to ride out the hardware-depreciation curve until investments in technology have been fully depreciated.

These factors make the ASP model a better fit for smaller companies, or new ventures within large companies, that don't have investment capital to spend on their own computing capacity. Smaller companies or new business ventures within larger companies can benefit from the ASP model, as long as they avoid the "day of reckoning", when I/T investment does not match business demand. They must decide when they will outgrow the ASP model and either move to totally outsource the I/T function, or develop the in-house capacity and I/T skills necessary to maintain revenue growth.

Chapter 5—Summary

This chapter began by describing two examples of how significant applications can determine the pace of business and in some cases, even how entire industries are run. Some of the most successful applications from a business perspective were designed in the 1960s and 1970s and are still running today. The chapter emphasized that successful application architecture is predicated on leveraging a few key software design concepts, with roots in the state-of-the-art within the I/T industry.

Next, the chapter described the N-Tier Software Framework and how it can extend business processes to customers, suppliers, and business partners. The model can be implemented with technology obtained from a number of different vendors. However, the key to successfully extending the enterprise is following the standards set by the most important standards bodies like the W3C and others.

The chapter concluded by discussing the roles that enterprise resource planning (ERP) software and the application service provider (ASP) models play in enterprise application architecture. ERP software vendors will continue to play an important role in shaping the future of I/T. However, linking ERP technology with in-house developed solutions using the N-Tier framework provides businesses with the most processing flexibility. The ASP model will continue to play a role for businesses wanting to mitigate the risks of new start-ups and provides the best economic benefits to companies with smaller I/T capital budgets.

The following chapter describes why information is the *product* of I/T, as well as the most important intangible asset of the enterprise. The chapter focuses on information at the "macro" level and how it contributes value to strategic business initiatives.

CHAPTER 6

Information Architecture

Information, information, information . . . it's what the technology hype is all about! Every program, data source, network device, and component of computer hardware exists to provide information to people and other systems. The enterprise thrives on using information to run operations, report on results, make sales, and control costs. It is very strange, then, that many companies have underinvested in the processes and systems to support the quality and control of their information. Many have problems finding their information, identifying how old it is, and knowing how to recover it in case of loss. This chapter focuses on how enterprise architecture can help a company manage and control its information, and use it strategically.

The Physics of Information

Information is a description of a person, place, thing, or an event which can be understood and consumed by people and machines. It is used by almost everyone within the business, by customers and suppliers. Information has properties that can be measured. These properties should be utilized to manage and govern how people use information. The properties of information include the following:

- identity—how is the information referenced?

78

- subject—what is the information about?
- validity—is the information from a trusted/certified source?
- freshness—is it out of date?
- context—is it a part other information?
- value—does it yield benefits to information consumers?
- dimension—is it complete?
- location—where is it kept and how can it be found?

Anything that can be digitized can be considered information. The process of capturing, encoding and storing information is relatively expensive. However, once digitized, reusing information in digital form is very inexpensive. By digitizing something, the digital information can be reused as many times as a business model dictates. Each time the information is reused, the relative unit cost of it drops.

By digitizing something from the physical world, the properties of the object change dramatically. Once becoming digital (or virtual), the properties that govern the object in the physical world no longer apply. Time and space (location) may no longer have the same effect on an object once it has been turned into a stream of bits.

Think of Google Earth. Once the entire earth was put into digital form, pictures of the planet down to a few yards of distance can be e-mailed anywhere instantly. By combining additional information like global positioning information with earth images, people can now see where they are, or get directions to anywhere in the world. By digitizing the pictures and GPS coordinates of the earth, Google created a new asset that did not exist before. By providing web links between earth information and merchant retailers, the new information asset formed the basis of a revenue generating product for Google. The Google search engine provides links to physical stores and online stores. Google generates revenue from placing these links in web pages associated with searches for store locations and for products. The company extended its base business model beyond providing search capabilities to consumers and businesses through the new location database and search engines of Google.

As information like GPS data from government satellites became readily reusable by companies like Google, other new products were developed, such as the GPS devices available in many vehicles today. The move to digitize objects has taken hold across the world, and smart business people are finding new ways to break the chains of the physical world and provide new value in the virtual world. Apple Inc. saw the value in digitizing music and its related information. Information related to music such as song title, band name, song writer and publisher have made the iPod and iTunes Music Store a complete success.

Much of the digital revolution has been made possible through extensive enhancements in data storage technologies. The independent research firm IDC reports that in 1999, the average cost of one gigabyte (one billion characters of data) of premium tier disk storage was $162.50. In 2006, the same amount of disk storage in the same class cost only $7.91 (IDC, "Worldwide Quarterly Disk Storage Systems Tracker", 2007—used by permission). That is over a 95 percent decrease in cost! This dramatic drop in storage costs was made possible through advancements in storage device technology, storage media, and the software that runs the storage systems. Since information is costing less and less to store, more and more of it is being captured, thereby driving up the *total* cost to the enterprise.

The increase in the amount of data being retained presents a new set of issues for the enterprise. The total cost of owning and controlling information has become a concern for many companies. As little as five years ago, companies may have kept between one and five terabytes (TB—one trillion characters of data) of information on file across the entire enterprise. Today, it is not uncommon for larger companies to have hundreds of TBs on file. How is such a vast amount of information kept current? How is it backed up and how long does it take to restore it? What about information that is stored as part of older systems that have been decommissioned or not kept up to date? What processes exist within the enterprise to manage, secure, and govern the use of the information? The remainder of this chapter holds the answers to these questions. It covers information management, data governance, and an introduction to data architecture.

Information Management

Companies have struggled over the years building, buying, installing, and running large complex applications. Some of the largest companies in the world have invested hundreds of millions of dollars in systems that accumulate information. Managing the vast amount of enterprise information is predicated on a combination of tools and governance procedures.

The tools used include a metadata repository, search technology tools, and reporting software tools. *Metadata* is data about data. For example, in the physical world, inventory stored in a warehouse is numbered, described, and cataloged so it can be easily found for shipping. Similarly, information is inventoried in the metadata repository of the enterprise. The figure below shows a logical view of a metadata repository and how it is integrated with the enterprise application architecture.

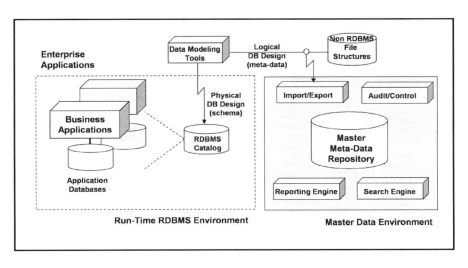

Figure 14—Master Metadata Environment

The *master metadata environment* acts as the inventory control system for data across the enterprise. The core of the environment is the master metadata repository. The repository is a database containing documentation about enterprise data.

There are two primary types of enterprise data. These are data stored in relational databases that are supported by relational database management systems (RDBMS) and other data not managed within an RDBMS. An example of non-relational data includes any file structure that is platform specific like Windows, Unix, and mainframe files. Files containing indexing schemes like VSAM or SAS files (SAS is a company engaged in development and marketing of data analysis and reporting technology) would be in the non-RDBMS classification.

Relational data is maintained by an RDBMS product such as Oracle, SQL Server, Sybase, DB2, and others. Each of these management systems has its own version of a catalog. The catalog contains information about the data stored and managed by the RDBMS. However, for the RDBMS and applications to work together, a format for the data must be specified, called a *schema*. The schema tells the RDBMS the names of the data fields in the database, whether they are numeric or character and other details about how data is managed by the RDBMS.

Database administrators (DBAs) develop schemas using tools that provide an easy way to configure the information for the RDBMS. DBAs use automation to create schemas that can be loaded into the RDBMS catalog. A specification called the data management language (DML) expressed in the form of Structured Query Language (SQL), tells the RDBMS about the data it will manage.

By tapping into the DML, information about what data is used by applications can be captured automatically and imported into the master metadata repository. Other processes are needed to capture and import data about non-RDBMS files because there is no standard DML available that describes them. Good master data environment products will provide automated ways to capture information about these non-RDBMS files. However, to make the information useful, people are required to manually enter additional details. Examples of metadata stored in the master repository include the following:

- data field (element) logical (business) name
- data field schema physical name

- data field description
- data field type (character, numeric, other)
- source of data field (which system created it)
- target of data field (which systems use it)
- data steward identifier (who has control over the field)
- encryption indicator (is the field required to be stored in encrypted format)
- valid values (list of what is valid for the field, if applicable)
- date entered into repository
- date last updated
- user ID of last update

Most good master metadata management products today contain even more information. This is just a representative sample of the data available in the metadata repository.

The search engine shown in Figure 14 can be used to explore information saved about enterprise data. It answers the questions, where is a particular field stored, who is responsible for maintaining it, where did it come from, and which systems use it? The reporting engine provides standard reports and can support ad-hoc reporting on the contents of the repository. The audit/control function maintains records of who added, updated, deleted, or accessed data within the repository. It also provides information to the reporting engine about possible redundant data fields and can identify areas of questionable information in the repository. Audit/control is an important feature of a master data environment as it can run analysis using the taxonomy of names and descriptions to find duplication before new data is added.

Storing the same metadata under different names will cause data integrity issues for anyone or any system attempting to use the repository. Lastly, the master data environment should contain various tools which data administrators can use to automate import and export processes. Importing data directly from data modeling tools saves time and increases accuracy. Exporting metadata to program code generation technologies called integrated development environments (IDEs) can speed up systems development time and improve testing quality.

Using the technology provided by a master data environment, the enterprise can develop a governance process to manage information effectively. Trying to manage the use and proliferation of information within and outside the enterprise without a master metadata environment would be like running a distribution center of finished goods inventory without an inventory control system. Policies and procedures for controlling the flow of finished goods into and out of the warehouse could be established but would lack the control processes to make sure they were being followed. Inventory in the warehouse would get lost, and no one would have a clear idea of where inventory was, where it came from, where it went, or who has received it.

No businessperson would try to run a warehouse without an inventory control system, so why would an enterprise run processes that are dependent on information without a control system? Many organizations have done this for years and are still successful. However, compliance laws and issues with unauthorized use of information, make it extremely difficult to manage information without formal investment in master data management tools and governance procedures. The master data environment is not all that is needed to effectively manage information. It must be coupled with a strong data governance process.

Data Governance

Chapter 3 described an enterprise architecture governance process. The process included the formation of an architecture review board (ARB), and an executive steering committee. It also defined roles of others that provide oversight to the activities of the committees. To manage the information within an enterprise, a similar governance construct is necessary. To be most effective, a master metadata environment should be in place before establishing any new data governance process. Attempting to establish the data governance body without the requisite tools will make it much more difficult for the governance team to perform its duties. However, for companies struggling with justification for the investment in infrastructure tools, establishing a data governance committee is better than doing nothing. The figure below shows how a committee can work to address data and information-related issues.

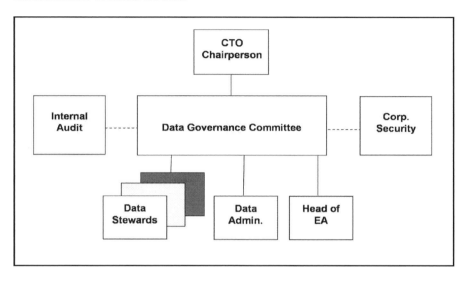

Figure 15—Data Governance Committee

A data governance committee should be chaired by a person with a background in I/T that understands the importance and challenges of managing information across the enterprise. This is typically the head of enterprise architecture, chief technology officer, head of data administration or, in some cases, the chief information officer of the company.

A critical success factor for a data governance process is the role of the *data steward*. Data stewards are people that usually work within business areas (non-I/T) that have responsibility for the quality and integrity of the information that their functional area creates and uses on a daily basis. Data stewards are representatives of others in the line of business and can make decisions about how data is named, defined, stored, and shared inside and outside the company. They are the final authority regarding the quality and integrity of the information they are responsible for.

Data stewards do not usually own and control the technology used to manage data. That is normally a function of people within I/T who develop data models or manage databases and files. Some companies combine teams that work on data modeling and database management, and others split them apart. Data modelers typically work at a logical level to describe the information needed to support automated business processes. Database administrators perform tasks associated with designing and maintaining databases at the physical level. Data stewards set the policies about data and help data modelers document those policies using the data modeling tools described above. Data stewards, data modelers, and database administrators all use the master metadata environment to help them perform their roles.

Data stewards also establish the rules regarding how data is secured. Must it be stored using encryption technology? Who is allowed to access and use the data? Data access rights are managed through a common repository of user IDs organized by roles. Typically, information about which users have which access rights is stored in the Lightweight Directory Access Protocol (LDAP) compliant repository of the company (See chapter 7 for more information about LDAP and security architecture in general).

While controlling who has rights to data, data stewards also control which companies and people are allowed to obtain and store data outside of the enterprise. A process should be established where data stewards must sign off and approve that data may be sent outside the enterprise to another company, or even a subsidiary of the enterprise. A log of which external companies received data should be maintained, and there should be policies in place about what other firms must do to protect the data once they have obtained it.

Must it be stored using encryption? Does the company need to keep track of who can access the data? Must it be destroyed at the end of its useful life? Does the enterprise which provided the data have the right to perform audits at the receiving enterprise? All these questions should be addressed by the policies set by the data governance committee. Data stewards are responsible for seeing that the policies are followed. The internal audit department should perform periodic audits to assure that policies are in place and are followed. Serious violations should be identified, and senior management should be informed of policy violations through their normal audit reporting processes.

Another key role of the data stewards and the governance committee is to gain consensus about the naming and meaning of data within the enterprise. This main function of the committee gives data the integrity needed to be reliable. The term quite often used for this is "a single source of truth." Many companies struggle with having redundant and misunderstood data. Something as simple as which time of day a specific data field was updated can have a major impact on its meaning.

Was the data field updated before a customer statement was prepared? Was it after the statement preparation date? Someone working on data analysis unaware of the timing impact could have performed analysis that was completely incorrect, stemming from that minor detail. If it was valid to view data before *and* after the statement date, then two different data fields would be required.

Each data field should be uniquely named. For example, one could establish two fields called "inter-cycle active balance" and "statement active balance." Both data fields store the "active balance." However, by naming them differently and using two different definitions for these fields in the master metadata repository, users will have a clear understanding of what data they are accessing for analytical and reporting purposes. Also, programmers working on systems development will know which data is which, when processing the "active balance" available in the database.

Combining management tools with procedures and policies aimed at governing the information of the enterprise provides the basis for building a data architecture. Business today runs at a fast pace and that pace is fueled through data. Without the tools and controls defined above, data may not be considered reliable information. Data alone is only a building block. It becomes *information* when the data is put into a context and has meaning for the people who consume it.

Data Architecture

Data can be organized into an architecture which provides business opportunities and process flexibility. This section focuses on the major categories of data that exist within the enterprise and how these categories can provide fuel to a business growth engine. It does not attempt to define how data should be organized or stored or managed within various technologies. There are many other sources available that describe building the data architecture. Our focus is on ways to think about data within the enterprise and how data can be organized to better serve the business.

By organizing data into specific classes, companies can make better decisions about managing data and find new ways to use data to run the business. Data can be classified as follows:

- *operational data*—obtained or created by a business process (automated and/or manual) and is used by, and for, business process automation.

- *analytic data*—originates from business operations or acquired outside of the normal business operation, but is used to perform analysis.

- *reporting data*—used to generate reports and provide data to information consumers through various means.

- *archival data*—saved for any reason by the business and can be recalled when needed.

Classifying data in this manner makes managing it easier and creates cost reduction opportunities. Table 4 below identifies the characteristics of each data classification.

Data Class	*Predominant Data Characteristics*
Operational Data	• Created, updated, accessed, and deleted by systems designed to run business processes. • Data is trusted as the truth. • Volumes (amount of data) are managed to assure systems run as intended. • Current according to the service levels of the business processes that create/use it. • Critical to the business processes and people who need and use it. • Could be accessed at a high rate of concurrency and often on a predictable basis. • Access to the data is tightly managed, and usage is closely controlled.
Analytic Data	• Copied from operational data, introduced from outside the organization, or derived during an analytic process. • Understood by those who perform analysis on behalf of the business. May or may not be treated as the source of truth. • Could be large in volume. • Current according to the service levels of the business processes that created it. • Must be available to the analytical processes that use it. Could be critical to business processes. • Access concurrency and timing is variable and unpredictable unless used by business processes. • Access is controlled, but usages are variable.
Reporting Data	• Copied from operational data and/or analytic data, introduced from outside the organization, or derived during an analytic or data-transformation process.

	• Understood by those who use reports. May be treated as the source of truth if the reports reflect data from operations without modification of content and context.
	• Current according to the service levels of the business processes that created the data used in the reports.
	• Must be available to the people and processes that use it according to when they need reports.
	• Generation of reports can be scheduled or on an as-needed basis or using self-service.
	• User level access controls exist.
Archival Data	• Data saved for historical purposes.
	• Can be large in volume.
	• Can become unusable over time.
	• Is used and accessed infrequently.
	• Could be recalled at any time for any reason.

Table 4—Data Classification Characteristics

By classifying data in this manner, I/T can match specific technologies to the data based on these characteristics, thereby optimizing management and access costs. For example, since archival data is large in volume and it is needed for historical purposes and accessed infrequently, it can be saved on the lowest cost storage media available. On the other hand, operational data is used to run the business directly and must be saved on storage media capable of keeping up with high rates of requests and updates performed randomly by people and machines doing their daily jobs. Analytic data, being large in volume but primarily accessed on an as-needed basis, need not be stored on the same high cost media used for operational data. Reporting data should be stored on media that is most appropriate for how it will be used. It can be kept in large lower cost files if reports are run in batch mode, and it can be stored in summarized form on higher performing media to meet the immediate access needs of management.

Matching data by classification with the appropriate hardware technology applies equally to data management software products. There are specialized products available for accessing all of these data classes. Traditional RDBMS products are used for operational data, and specialized engines that apply parallel processing architectures can be used with analytic data. There are many products on the market that perform and enable reporting. Other products have been designed to address the archival data classification. There are also tools and products available that move data from one classification to another. These are called *extract transformation and load* (ETL) tools. ETL tools help to put data into the correct formats as it moves from one classification to another and the ability to summarize details into higher-level values.

The figure below shows how the various classes of data are organized to form the *enterprise data architecture*. This architecture shows how data used in operational business systems relates to the other data classifications.

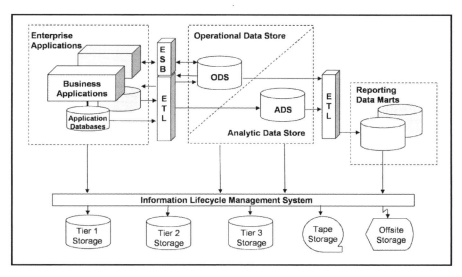

Figure 16—Enterprise Data Architecture

Figure 16 shows data being replicated into multiple classes. As data is copied, it is usually organized differently to meet the different sets of requirements, or characteristics, associated with how the data will be utilized. Data used by applications is moved by ETL tools into an *operational data store* (ODS).

The ODS records the events of the business and is a place where an enterprise view can be developed of these events across lines of businesses. To meet business service levels associated with applications, the ODS will only contain data that is current and relevant to the daily, weekly, or monthly events of the enterprise. Therefore, data within the ODS is stored in a non-summarized format and is not more than between one and three years old. Most often, the data in the ODS is from the last quarter or possibility up to four contiguous quarters. The key characteristic of the ODS is that it is directly involved in the daily routine of running applications. Therefore, moving data into and taking data back out from the ODS, must be an efficient process, taking only a few hours.

More advanced implementations of the ODS may include a "trigger" mechanism. Triggers are set within applications and when tripped, a message containing data used within an application is sent into the ODS via an enterprise service bus (ESB). The ESB is explained in more detail within chapter 10 Service-Oriented Architecture. However, for the purposes of the data architecture, the ESB is an online real time transport mechanism between the applications of the enterprise and the ODS.

Whether the ESB is used or not, data must be moved using an ETL tool from application data sources into the ODS. By copying data in this controlled manner, service levels established for the applications can be met, and there is no single point of failure for business applications. The ODS provides a central location where data is saved outside of the context from which it was originated. This is important, as each application may use data differently within a different context.

Typically, but not in all cases, the ODS will feed data back into operational application data stores using the ETL tool. In this way, data that may have been captured across the business can be used by systems involved in decision making on behalf of customers, suppliers, and business partners.

The ODS must meet the strict service levels of applications used to run the business and is not normally stored in a format making ad-hoc analysis easy to perform. Business leaders who want to ask "what if" questions may need much more information in the form of history than what is available from the ODS. Also, analysts may want to mix new data sources found outside the company together with data used within the enterprise to find new trends, make hypothesis, and confirm hypothesis. All of these non-operational requirements create the need for an *analytic data store* (ADS).

The ADS is used by people in the business looking to introduce new products, find new market opportunities, and make new business proposals. Users of the ADS want access to vast amounts of data and quick turn around on their requests and queries. Analysts typically are not authorized to affect the applications of the business directly, as they work on new products and proposals for management. They may create new data, called *derived data,* but they should not be able to introduce the derived data directly into applications without data governance committee approval and support from the I/T areas that support applications. Adding new data to business processes, and the applications that support them, usually requires I/T to create or modify programs, making the new data a part of the daily processing and business processes of the enterprise.

Because data stored in the ADS is large in volume and uses of the data cannot be scheduled, the base technology required for the ADS must be scalable. It must be able to scale quickly to process queries that span billions of records (rows) and provide answers to the user community in a reasonable amount of time.

Scalability requirements differ between the ODS and the ADS. It is possible to leverage the same technology to support both the ODS and ADS, but the technology must be able to meet the daily needs of a strict level of service *and* respond to a wide range of ad hoc requests. Since the amount of data flowing into and out from the ODS is controlled by the daily processing schedule of applications, the ability to quickly expand the amount of storage available and processing power is not a major requirement.

The ODS can be expanded on a biannual or annual basis. On the other hand, the amount of data to be loaded into the ADS is unpredictable, as is the timing of ad hoc queries. Therefore, the technology used to support the ADS must be easily scalable without the need to logically reorganize the data already present within the database.

Even though large amounts of data are saved in the ADS, it is not stored in summarized format. This makes data in the ADS difficult to use for business reporting purposes. Therefore, many organizations use ETL to migrate and summarize data from either the ODS and/or the ADS and build *data marts* for reporting purposes.

Data marts contain data that has been summarized for a particular use and can be specific to the line of business needing information. Data marts are the locations in the enterprise data architecture where data takes on the context of the business. There is typically a mixture of reports that management needs to keep track of business events. Business people cannot sift though millions or billions of records of detail; therefore, data is summarized within data marts to make it faster to access and easier to use. There are a number of products available that summarize data. Some products are able to combine detail from the ODS/ADS with summarized data to provide even more insight to management. Also, by placing data into predefined formats in summary form, business people can serve themselves more easily. This requires less or, in many cases, no programming help from I/T.

As Figure 16 shows, all classifications of data must be saved and be recoverable. An *information lifecycle management* (ILM) system is used to perform back up and recovery of data. The ILM takes responsibility for placing data into the most cost-effective media while still meeting all regulatory and disaster recovery requirements. The most expensive media is used to backup data used by applications. Less expensive media is used for the ODS and ADS, and lastly, the least expensive media is used to archive data for historical purposes. ILM solutions can be purchased from a single vendor or from a number of vendors. Polices regarding the retention of data must be set by the data stewards and carried out by a combination of systems and I/T administrators. ILM technology can assure that data management polices are enforced, as information moves from one classification to another.

Chapter 6—Summary

This chapter described the need for an enterprise metadata environment and how it enables the data governance process. The enterprise metadata environment and data governance process provide management tools for supporting the vast amount of information created within today's enterprise. The entire ecosystem needed to support data at the enterprise level is not inexpensive, but given the level of dependency businesses have on data, an investment in the underlying technologies is necessary for a well managed data environment.

Through classifying data by its characteristics, I/T can reduce the total cost associated with managing huge amounts of data. Also, by introducing effective ways to move data through various data classifications, the enterprise can create new products, open new markets, and expand operations without repeatedly reorganizing the systems and business processes of the company. The chapter concluded with a brief introduction to the enterprise data architecture. Basic database structures required to meet various service levels were introduced and a mechanism to move data through its life cycle was presented.

The next chapter explores how networks act as the "circulatory system" of a company, linking data stores to applications and providing the mechanism for business growth.

CHAPTER 7

Network Architecture

While information fuels the business, networks enable growth. Just as the circulatory system determines the pace at which the human body functions, networks support the rate of growth of the enterprise. The faster information can move through the enterprise, the faster customers can be serviced, orders sent to suppliers, and partners retained. The more quickly information can move within and outside the enterprise, the more efficiently the enterprise runs. This chapter covers the basic evolution of network architecture and a description of how various networks can be combined to form new products and services. It also discusses network security architecture and directory services at a high level.

Evolution to a Single Standard

In the past, most networks were either inside a company, agency, or university in the form of wide area networks (WANs) or local area networks (LANs). Today, cellular networks, wireless networks (Wi-Fi), and the Internet offer new opportunities for companies to build and deliver new products and services never before imagined. The digital revolution, as evidenced by the ubiquitous adoption of the Internet on a worldwide scale, would not be happening without the major advancements in networking technology.

The introduction of the mainframe computer and online access created the need for attaching terminals through a network. In the earliest days of computing, most processing was done in the back room, so to speak, on large computers capable of processing records in sequence. It became evident that users needed to access information outside of the traditional reports they received from the mailroom each day, and terminals were invented.

IBM developed networks to allow terminals (called 3270 terminals, after the data communication protocol used to connect to the mainframe) to provide people with online access to data. Systems such as VTAM, CICS, and IMS provided users with easy to use online access to data. These early online systems were developed based on a hierarchical control model that assumed all data was resident on centralized computers (mainframes). The hierarchical network of IBM's Systems Network Architecture (SNA) was a success from the 1970s into the early 1990s, and every company with an IBM mainframe used SNA. At the same time SNA was meeting networking needs within companies around the world, work was being done by the founders of what would eventually become the Internet.

The United States Government formed what was known as the Defense Advanced Research Project Agency (DARPA) in 1957, in response to the Soviet launch of the first satellite, Sputnik I. DARPA worked on developing various new technological advancements including ways to connect computer systems using radio and landline telephony architecture. In 1968-69, DARPA formed what was called the ARPANET. ARPANET linked computers from various government agencies across the United States and was designed to support packet-switching network architecture. ARPANET expanded across many government agencies, and through linkages with universities around the world, spread beyond the U.S. Government. Public expansion continued as individuals and businesses connected to the world wide network. Due its massive popularity and the fact that business was becoming dependent on it, the US Government turned over control of the network hubs to independent organizations in 1995, forming the Internet we know today.

The critical technological advancement that ultimately formed the Internet was the development of common peer-to-peer communication standards. TCP/IP was developed by Robert Kahn, Vinton Cref, and others in the early 1980s. TCP/IP made it possible for the network to grow without bounds by being the standard for all data transport over the Internet. People and businesses could join the Internet without worrying about being charged fees or being controlled by a single company or government agency. The inherent network architecture of the Internet, based on a peer-to-peer routing scheme, made this possible.

At the same time the Internet was expanding, the PC was brought to market by IBM and Apple in 1981. These new computers needed access to shared services and other PCs. Personal computers and dedicated computing equipment, like word processors, required people to share data, files, and printing services. Local area network architectures were developed to address these requirements from companies like IBM (Token Ring) and Xerox (Ethernet).

For years, these network solutions (Token Ring and Ethernet) coexisted, and companies large and small adopted one or both of these technologies. IBM even introduced a peer-to-peer network architecture in the late 1980s based on their very successful midrange computing platform, the AS400. It employed a peer-to-peer networking scheme called low-entry networking (LEN). Today, Token-Ring LANs are basically extinct, and most companies, if not all, have adopted Ethernet as their standard LAN network technology. There are a number of factors behind Ethernet emerging as the predominant LAN solution for businesses, but support for TCP/IP and higher transmission bandwidths over lower cost coaxial cables and twisted pair phone wires were the differentiators.

Out of this evolution, over the past thirty years or so, one network model emerged as the standard for connecting computers and terminals. TCP/IP has become the standard network protocol across the world today because of how it was architected from inception. TCP/IP networks do not assume there is any single control point or computer hub. They work by having the routing and control programs needed for transmitting data on all end points in the network (called nodes). Each node is an active participant in the never-ending chain of interconnected computers. This architecture construct made TCP/IP naturally scalable, and since it was based on standards developed by open standards bodies, no one company could control how it worked. By adopting TCP/IP, network equipment companies and computer companies were confident their products would be interoperable.

Over the years, various network solutions were created to address long distance data connectivity. These networks were designed to move TCP/IP and other protocol traffic. They include X.25 (data packet switching over private lines at a predefined transfer rate); integrated services digital network (ISDN) (dedicated circuit over public lines at a predefined transfer rate); frame relay (dedicated circuits over private lines with transmission bursts supported to a committed information rate); and asynchronous transfer mode (ATM) (dedicated circuits over private lines with variable transfer rates and quality-of-service). Quality-of-service (QoS) refers to technology allowing network administrators to assign various routing priorities to different types of network transmissions.

Each of these network architectures has its strengths and weaknesses, and each was introduced to address the shortcomings of the predecessor. X.25 relays messages well, but has problems meeting reliability requirements, does not scale up as demands increase and has bandwidth limitations. ISDN provides dedicated bandwidth over existing telephone lines. However, ISDN does not scale as demand increases and has bandwidth limitations. Frame relay provides consistent generalized service levels using dedicated network circuits and can automatically adjust transfer rates as demand increases up to a predefined limit. ATM supports dynamically scalable capacity, can differentiate information transfer by type, and has QoS management capabilities.

The next evolution for wide area networking within companies is multiprotocol label switching (MPLS). MPLS is quickly becoming an important technology to the expansion of virtual private networks (VPNs) because it provides comprehensive QoS services reaching to all endpoints in the network. MPLS is highly scalable and differentiates end-to-end TCP/IP services requiring less management attention and technical infrastructure than ATM or Frame Relay alone.

Another major evolution in network architecture is the emergence of voice-over-IP (VOIP). As discussed in the chapter on data architecture, anything that is digitized can be passed over networks, transcending space and time. Voice used to be transmitted in analog form over phone lines, but because TCP/IP has become a common data transmission protocol, the invention of technology to convert analog voice signals into digital TCP/IP messages (packets) created a whole new medium for transmitting conversations.

VOIP is a disruptive technology because the Internet can be used in place of the private landline networks of the past, to transmit conversations across the world. Using VOIP, calls can be made for free over the Internet using TCP/IP as the messaging protocol. Free in this case, means no additional charges for the voice connection. There are fees associated with the Internet connection but these are not billed the same way as are voice connections using the plain-old-telephone-system (POTS). This event, along with the introduction of cellular networks, is transforming the telecommunications industry.

Wireless Comes of Age

Wireless technology has evolved rapidly over the past few years and has been connected to the Internet to form an entirely new mode of computing. Wireless networks began as analog and evolved into digital packet data networks. While there are various technologies employed by various firms, all have adopted TCP/IP as their overall communications protocol, making them interoperable with their landline predecessors.

Cellular networks evolved from research performed on the convergence of radio wave technology with computer technology. Radio signals were the transport mechanism instead of wires, and telecommunications equipment translated analog signals into digital signals for computer consumption. In today's world, there are numerous solutions available connecting people and computers using the airwaves. Some of the more important wireless network solutions available are:

- CDMA-code division multiple access
- EGPRS (3G)/EDGE-enhanced data rates for GSM evolution
- GPRS-general packet radio service
- GSM-global system for mobile communications
- Mobitex-pager-based network in USA and Canada
- NFC-near field communications
- PCS-personal communication system
- RFID-radio frequency identification
- TDMA (2G)-time division multiple access
- UMTS (3G)-universal mobile telecommunications system
- W-CDMA-wideband code division multiple access
- Wireless LAN-local area network (Wi-Fi)
- Wireless MAN-metropolitan area network (Wi-Max)
- Wireless PAN-personal area network (Bluetooth)

Describing each of these in detail and identifying the differences between them is not the main focus here. However, there are major wireless-networking models that deserve the attention of anyone engaged in bringing new products to market using the advanced features of wireless networks.

Global system for mobile communications (GSM) is the most popular standard for mobile phones in the world. GSM service is used by over two billion people across more than 200 countries and territories. GSM is typically used to deliver a mobile service called general packet radio service (GPRS). GPRS is a data transfer service offered by many cellular carriers for mobile data transmissions. These mobile data transmission services include TCP/IP, http, the wireless access protocol (WAP), short message service (SMS), and multimedia messaging service (MMS). All of these services are available today to millions of subscribers on a worldwide scale.

The wireless access protocol (WAP) is a data transfer standard based on an extended form of html. Using the browser within a mobile device, people can obtain access to the Internet over cellular networks. Short message service (SMS) is a near real-time message relay service. It allows people to send and receive text messages of up to 160 characters in length. Multimedia messaging service (MMS) allows people to send and receive digital images and digital video over cellular networks.

GSM and GPRS are called second generation or 2G network solutions, as they have service and bandwidth limitations. In 2003, an enhancement to GPRS was created called EDGE, also referred to as EGPRS. EDGE stands for enhanced data rates for GSM evolution. EDGE is typically called a 2.5G network, as it improves transmission rates and reliability over what is provided by 2G. EDGE has been used successfully in PDA solutions where a higher rate of throughput is needed with greater reliability than basic GPRS for wireless data transmission.

At the same time GSM was being introduced on a worldwide scale, a competing wireless set of standards were also taking hold. The alternative cellular network technology is code division multiple access (CDMA). CDMA was developed by Qualcomm and was adopted by some of the largest cellular network operators in the world. Like GSM/GPRS, CDMA also supports WAP, SMS and MMS messaging types. CDMA was later enhanced to increase overall bandwidth and is now called wideband code division multiple access (WCDMA).

GSM was developed as a complete technical architecture supporting wireless communications, a "turn-key" solution for cellular operators. WCMDA is based on a set of standards similar to that of GSM, but WCDMA allows cellular operators to build customized services on a standards base. Each of the two cellular networking architectures has its own unique characteristics. For example, cell phones on the GSM architecture use SIM chips to store the cellular network address, phone number, and subscriber personal data. Cell phones designed to run on a WCDMA network do not use SIM chips and instead store identifying information within the cellular network. WCDMA devices do have an integrated circuit embedded in the phone's architecture where personal information can be saved locally.

Due in part to these two different cellular network architectures, a person cannot take a device designed for a GSM network and use it unaltered on a WCDMA network, and vice versa. In fact, when a person purchases a phone, or other wireless device, from a cellular operator directly, the device is normally "locked" by the operator. Locking the device means that it cannot run on any other cellular network unless it is "unlocked". Unlocking a wireless device is not a simple process that most consumers can do by themselves.

Another important difference between GSM and WCDMA is the application software that can be installed on phones and other devices designed for these two different networks. Phones designed to run on a GSM network support the Sun Microsystems developed, Java 2 Mobile Edition (J2ME) run-time system. Programmers can license the J2ME System Development Kit (SDK) and build applications that can be downloaded by cellular subscribers without the involvement of third parties.

While the combination of GSM and J2ME is open to software developers, GSM based cellular operators have some control over the software allowed on handsets they sell. Applications downloaded by consumers that have not been certified by cellular operators will be treated by the cell phone as "untrusted applications". The phone's operating system will intervene with a message to the cell phone user every time the "rogue" application is opened. In addition, these applications are not easy to find on the phone's menu system, making them more difficult for consumers to use.

Phones designed to run on WCDMA networks use the Qualcomm developed, BREW Client run-time system. To develop an application for a WCDMA handset/device, the programmer must obtain a license to the BREW SDK. The BREW SDK supports coding in Java but generates a different set of bytecode compatible with the BREW run-time system rather than the J2ME run-time system. Due to the proprietary architecture of WCDMA networks, Qualcomm must "certify" BREW applications before they can be adopted by cellular operators. Because BREW applications must be certified by Qualcomm, subscribers on WCDMA networks cannot download applications from non-certified software providers. Cellular operators of WCDMA networks have full control over the software targeted for wireless devices on their networks.

Microsoft Windows Mobile is certified for specific devices by cellular operators in advance of those devices being sold to the public. Mobile devices sold with Windows Mobile support subscriber direct application downloads. The number of devices approved to run Windows Mobile has been limited in the past to PDAs and smartphones, which limited its reach as compared with J2ME and BREW. As hardware and software technology of wireless devices improves, Windows Mobile will be preinstalled on more of them. This will open a larger market for application providers for Windows Mobile. Since the base software layer, Windows Mobile, is certified by the cellular operator, almost any mobile application can be made available directly to the public without intervention of the cellular operator who originally sold the device to the subscriber/consumer.

It is possible for companies to provide mobile access to their private systems without the direct involvement of cellular operators. The two primary methods involve leveraging SMS and the mobile browser included in most wireless devices.

SMS was first introduced by cellular operators as an add-on feature of wireless devices and their networks. The first implementations of SMS were closed to the networks who offered the service. To solve the problem of cross-network text messaging, intermediary companies emerged, providing inter-network SMS switching services. Mobile intermediaries can deliver better service levels and can aggregate usage across cellular operators. They act like internet server providers (ISPs) in the value chain for mobile messaging.

Intermediaries make using SMS feasible for companies with large numbers of customers. However, the message length limitation of 160 characters restricts application functionality. Companies interested in reaching their customers over cellular networks can do so without working directly with cellular operators by using SMS, but they will need to work through an intermediary which does have a direct relationship.

The second open mobile access approach available is leveraging the mobile browser software included with most mobile devices. The mobile web browser uses http over TCP/IP for data communications over the cellular network. As mentioned earlier, both GSM/GPRS and WCDMA networks support these data communications standards. Customers with mobile devices can use the web browser on their device to access a smaller version of a company's website. By developing a website to support extensible hypertext markup language (xhtml), companies can bypass the need for SMS intermediaries and cellular operators.

The W3C adopted the wireless access protocol (WAP) and enhanced the original standards with xhtml to form WAP 2.0. Since using a website typically requires quite a bit of typing, solutions that rely on the mobile device's web browser will also have limited functionality. Businesses that have developed their websites to support WAP 2.0 do not need the approval of the cellular operator to offer mobile access to their customers.

The introduction of the iPhone by Apple, Inc. in 2007 could be a milestone for mobile applications. Since the iPhone includes touch screen technology, use of the web browser included with the iPhone makes navigating web sites much easier than from the limited key pad of a traditional cell phone. Companies wanting the robust functionality offered from their Internet sites may be able to offer virtually the same capabilities to mobile customers without needing an intermediary or working directly with cellular operators. Of course access to the Internet, regardless of the wireless networking model, must utilize a data service plan offered by a cellular company or an agent of a cellular company.

GSM and WCDMA networks are converging to a third generation architecture called 3G. The main standards body responsible for defining mobile 3G standards is the 3rd Generation Partnership Project (3GPP), which is a joint effort of several standards groups around the world. The project is focused on creating a new converged set of standards called universal mobile telecommunications system (UMTS).

3G technologies (UMTS) enable network operators to offer subscribers a wider range of advanced services, with greater network capacity, at a lower operating cost. Services include both wide-area wireless voice telephony and broadband wireless data, in a mobile environment. While cellular operators are moving toward the 3G standard, it takes time for all the devices in the network to turn over to newer devices that support 3G technology. Therefore, there are devices being used across the world that support 2G, 2.5G, and 3G standards. Over time, 3G technology will phase out the older technologies and all operators will adopt a cellular network architecture based on the same standards.

Personal and local wireless networks based on wireless standards are being adopted at a fast pace. These include those that support the IEEE 802.15.1 (Bluetooth) standard, also known as the personal area network, and IEEE 802.11, also known as wireless LAN and Wi-Fi. These two play roles in the overall networking ecosystem as end point connections. People walking around with earbuds seemingly talking to themselves are using Bluetooth, and many people have installed wireless LANs in their homes and businesses.

The lowest frequency radio networks available are RFID (radio frequency identification) and NFC (near-field communications). RFID is used to send and receive small amounts of data over a specific frequency and is usually associated with inventory control. RFID is designed to utilize a limited radio spectrum and is restricted to a few meters in distance. RFID is used primarily in inventory control and logistics solutions for asset tracking. RFID is also being used with smart-card technology to pass personal information to RFID-enabled readers.

NFC is also a low frequency radio technology. It is used in various applications where a smart chip can process data at the local source of the message. NFC has an even more limited transmission range of only a few centimeters making it more secure than RFID in certain applications. NFC chips are being used in smart-card applications of all types and are even being placed into cell phones and other devices to securely store and transmit debit and credit card information.

A device equipped with either an RFID chip or an NFC chip and complementary antenna can communicate using the ISO 14443 standard for contactless messaging with readers tuned to the appropriate frequency. Technologies like Bluetooth, RFID and NFC create a new *micro-network architecture* where new products can be introduced to the market. Connecting micro-networks with Wi-Fi, Wi-Max, cellular, satellite and the Internet, creates a new opportunity for wireless solutions of all kinds. Companies looking to expand their product horizons cannot afford to ignore the new channels created by mobile and wireless technology.

The Other Network

Almost everyone knows about the Internet, and many people use it daily. Anyone working in a major corporation uses their company private network each day. We see almost everyone now using a cell phone or other wireless device to communicate. However, there is another network most people use on a daily basis but almost never think about. That network has become an integral part of almost everyone's lives and sits in the background silently enabling commerce on a massive scale. This "other network" is the *payment network*. Actually, there are many payment networks, but taken together, they enable commerce on a global scale.

Payment networks link millions of merchants to processors and banks and handle billions in spending, money transfer, and other transactions around the globe. The most notable private payment networks have been developed by American Express (AMEX), Discover, MasterCard, and VISA. Other important payment networks include Diners Club International, China UnionPay (CUP), Link and JCB. Companies such as PayPal, Google and others have entered the payments business to some degree, but they still rely on the payment networks listed to handle credit payment transactions.

Traditional payment networks work by using a system of routing numbers. These are called *bank identification numbers* or BINs. The BIN is the first (left most) six digits of the account number on any credit or debit card. The International

Organization for Standardization (ISO) has assigned and controls ranges of these BINs (ISO 7812 standard) to payment network companies and card issuing banks.

The unique combination of numbers within the "BIN range", enable routing of payment transactions (debit or credit) through the proper payment network to the bank/lender who issued the card. Routing tables stored within the payment networks are updated on a periodic basis. Each payment network has a schedule for times during the year when tables can be updated. Update schedules are different for each network across the world so making a new range active on a world wide scale may take more than one year.

There are also many entities in the payment network value chain that process payment transactions. These include companies that sell and service point-of-sale card readers, transaction acquirers and card account processors. These entities all rely on the BIN range to determine which bank/lender a transaction applies to. Changing these systems to support new BIN ranges is difficult to coordinate, especially across major payment networks and across geographies and could take many years to complete on a large scale.

Because of the time to update point-of-sale terminals, payment routing tables and processing systems with new BINs, new entrants to the payments business rarely succeed. The industry calls this the "chicken and egg problem". Payment devices or products that require new BINs won't be available to the masses until all merchants have updated their terminals. Merchants won't update their terminals until there is a critical mass of payment devices with the new BINs. Therefore, to assure they can accept payments from as many customers as possible, merchants subscribe to the established payment networks.

Even though web based businesses do not have payment terminals where cards are swiped, the connection to the customer's bank account or credit account is still driven by BIN range. So the "chicken and egg problem" also applies to any web business that wishes to accept credit transactions. Web based merchants located in the United States and in some other countries can process non-credit transactions through the Automated Clearing House (ACH).

The ACH was established by the United States Federal Reserve to enable money movement between member banks in the USA and overseas. Although the ACH was established to enable the monetary system in the USA (especially for check payments), it is now being exploited as a low cost and secure service provider for any business wanting to electronically present payments against customer's checking accounts (debit transactions). The ACH also has a routing number scheme. The combination of the bank routing number and account number at the bottom of all checks controls how transactions flow to banks through the ACH. Therefore, online bill payment works because consumers can load their own routing information into a web page and funds will be routed from their checking accounts over the ACH to the appropriate merchant. From a consumer point of view, these payments can only be processed from a checking account.

Because the ACH works in what is known as "offline mode," there is always the risk that a customer's checking account will not have the funds available to process a payment. In this case, the payment processor or merchant will take the financial risk of a non-sufficient funds scenario. This risk can be substantial if the payment network or merchant handles high volumes of ACH transactions. To make sure funds are available, or to process a credit transaction, new payment network providers must obtain rights to the BIN range offered by a private payment network.

Why discuss payment networks in a book about enterprise architecture? Because new business opportunities can be created by linking the Internet, cellular networks and payment networks into a holistic solution for consumers and businesses. The Internet enabled online customer service, web-based statements, web-based complaint handling, online banking, and many more services. Cellular networks open these services to people in a new way as each person possesses a unique address in the form of their cellular number and carries an always-on device at all times.

By linking payment capabilities with mobile networks consumers can do almost anything they can from a PC, ATM, or at a store, using their wireless device.

There are limits to what can be done from a wireless device, but as more and more physical things are rendered digitally, people will have more ways to conduct business. As figure 17 shows, people with the appropriate technology on their mobile device would not have to actually visit an ATM to obtain cash. They could simply request a refresh of cash into a virtual account issued within a valid BIN range.

Using an NFC-enabled phone they could spend the virtual cash at a merchant equipped with an RFID-enabled point-of-sale terminal. By digitizing the BIN information that is normally on a payment card, a cell phone can be used to make a payment. NFC sends a wireless message a few centimeters from the phone to the RFID enabled reader at the merchant. From this point forward, the payment message looks and behaves as if the plastic card were "swiped" at the merchant's point-of-sale terminal. NFC and the RFID enabled reader break the bond of the card form factor, allowing almost any device to become a "payment card". A variation of this example would be to use the phone to request the cash refresh, but the consumer would have a card that was issued which corresponds with the virtual account.

Similarly, people could send money to others who are "in network" by sending a message from their wireless device to a clearing agent. The clearing agent would assure the identity of the sending and receiving parties and process the transfer from one account to the other within the same system or outside the system by using the ACH or a traditional payment network. The enabling technologies are all readily available, and by converging the Internet, wireless networks and payment networks, value added services can be generated, yielding new revenue opportunities.

Figure 17 shows how these three networks can logically converge from an architecture perspective to build new services that were once only available within a specific networking channel.

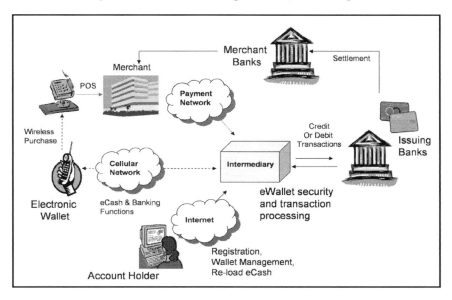

Figure 17—Example of Converging Networks

In this example, the Internet provides a complete user interface for registration, product selection, and setting up the messages a consumer would like to subscribe to, once their cell phone is enabled with an eWallet application. The cellular network provides support for real-time access to account information. In this case, the transaction set supported by the ecosystem includes obtaining electronic cash. The eCash can be moved into a clearing account that is associated with a traditional card containing a magnetic stripe, or an RFID enabled card, or an NFC-enabled cell phone.

To spend the eCash, the consumer swipes the card, or waves their card or cell phone near an RFID-enabled point-of-sale terminal at a merchant. In the case of an NFC payment, software loaded on the RF-enabled point-of-sale terminal converts the ISO compliant (ISO 14443 wireless protocol standard) wireless message that came from the NFC-enabled device into a traditional payment message (ISO 8583 payment message format). Once the payment message has been created by the point-of-sale device, it can be processed through the existing payment networks and processed by the bank which issued the card or enabled the NFC-enabled phone.

Figure 17 shows how new business value and solutions can be generated by linking three different networks into a single business solution. By adding the other networks described, such as a personal area network (Bluetooth) and/or Wi-Fi connectivity, other innovative solutions can also be developed.

Security Architecture

Since security is involved with protecting access to networks, the security architecture can be included in a description of network architecture. Firewalls are part of the network design, and systems related to user authentication are aligned with networking technologies. Managing security for systems and data within the enterprise is a balancing act between providing access and barring access. At an extreme, the most secure system would not allow any person or system external to the enterprise to access data or applications inside the enterprise. Of course, barring all access defeats the purpose of using systems for business benefit, so by definition, access must be managed not blocked. Therefore, the role of well-designed security architecture is to allow access to systems and data using a set of rules and providing filters to stop unauthorized access.

The mainstay of any well-designed security architecture is placing control points in the network where messages can be allowed, blocked, or managed as they flow through the network. This is normally accomplished by setting up security zones within the company's network. Firewalls are used to divide the network into these zones. Figure 18 shows there are usually three zones established to manage transaction and messaging traffic.

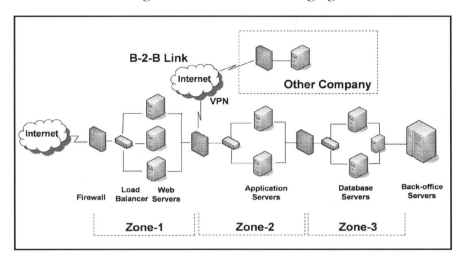

Figure 18—Security Architecture

Zone 1 is where web servers reside, facing the outside world. Web servers placed in Zone 1 allow access to public information, and until a person has been authenticated will not allow access to systems placed in Zone 2. Systems placed in Zone 2 may include web servers containing private data or application servers that use private data in the course of providing a business process to the outside world. Systems placed in Zone 3 contain database servers that provide private data and may include network access between applications in Zone 2 and other applications that are inside the corporate network. Depending on the philosophy of the security group within the enterprise, firewalls may be used to segment access to business systems running across untrusted networks that reside within the company. Untrusted networks may be owned and operated by the enterprise, but there may be no centralized control over data and systems running across the internal network. B2B connections are usually set up as virtual private networks (VPNs). VPNs are virtual networks established either over privately managed lines or, more typically, using the Internet to connect companies. VPNs utilize ISO compliant security standards and are established with both companies agreeing on firewall rules and transmission encryption standards.

Directory service architecture is closely related to the overall security architecture of the enterprise. While firewalls protect access to networks and platforms, directories protect access to applications and other components of the technology infrastructure. Directories contain user IDs, user passwords, and access rights for the enterprise. Directory services of today have evolved from a set of standards developed by ISO and the International Telecommunications Union (ITU). The specifications called the X.500 standards, were first published by the ISO/ITU in 1988 and revised in 1993 and 1997. As shown in table 5, there are a number of standards that are all part of the overall X.500 framework.

Doc. Num.	Title	Published
X.500	The Directory: overview, concepts, models, and services	1988
X.501	Models	1988
X.509	Authentication framework	1988
X.511	Abstract service definition	1988
X.518	Procedures for distributed operation	1988
X.519	Protocol specifications	1988
X.520	Selected attribute types	1988
X.521	Selected object classes	1988
X.525	Replication	1993
X.530	Use of systems management for admin. of directory	1997

Table 5—The X.500 Standards

The establishment of open standards that make up X.500 specifications was an important milestone for security. However, the specifications of the access protocol into the X.500 directory information base (DIB) were not widely adopted, partly because they did not require a TCP/IP transportation layer. Therefore, the ISO Development Environment (ISODE) at the University of Michigan developed an easy to implement, TCP/IP-based, access protocol to replace the X.500 directory access protocol (DAP). The new protocol was named lightweight directory access protocol (LDAP). Since the introduction of version 3 of LDAP in 1995, the new directory architecture has become almost universal.

Since LDAP is based on the X.500 specifications, it retained the attributes of a hierarchical information base, domain name service, and distributed directory information bases. However, the internal data model for LDAP is based on an extensible schema allowing companies to augment basic "out of the box" objects, without impacting the overall directory service operational model.

Microsoft, Sun Microsystems, and IBM have developed their own security and authentication technologies based on the X.500 standards. Each also adopted the base set of LDAP standards and made modifications to meet their individual product plans. Many companies have adopted technology developed by these three companies to manage their security and directory infrastructures. Some of these products are shown in figure 19. The figure represents an example of how directory architecture can meet the security requirements of the enterprise. It provides a logical view into security architecture. Companies implement directory and security architectures according to their unique policies and may be different than the example.

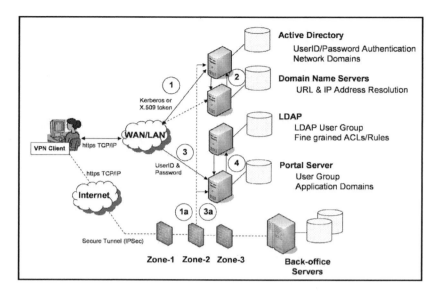

Figure 19—Basic Directory Architecture

This sample directory architecture shows how Active Directory (part of the Microsoft security suite), can work with a SUN LDAP Server from Sun Microsystems and an IBM Websphere Portal Server. The numbered data flows indicate the integration process between these systems at the time an authorized person attempts to sign on to their applications. The sign-on process begins at the user's desktop with the log-on against the local Active Directory (AD) client.

Flow 1—AD uses the user ID and password to create a kerberos compliant token, and passes the token to the AD server. Kerberos is a type of encryption standard used to secure ids and passwords.

Flow 2—The AD server calls into the domain name server (DNS) to obtain which network domains are valid for the token (user).

Flow 3—After the system responds with acceptance for the user, the user sends a request into the portal server passing the user ID and password over an https connection. (This step could be streamlined by introducing a single sign-on (SSO) architecture which adds complexity). The portal server identifies the appropriate user group and determines which applications are allowed for the user.

Flow 4—If a set of detailed access control lists (ACLs) or security rules exist at the application level, a call is made from the portal server to the LDAP directory. The ACLs that are valid for the user group along with any detailed rules that may exist on the LDAP database are presented to the application.

The flows are a bit different in the case of a user attempting to sign on across the Internet. In that case, the https request must pass through Zones 1 and 2 before gaining access to the Active Directory server. A secure tunnel is established between a VPN client and the Zone 1 firewall using https and IPSec (IP Security) to maintain security over the web for the sign-on and access to all other back-office servers.

There are many variations of this architecture, and the final design will be established by the information security group within the enterprise. This particular model is a high-level view into what is possible. Not all companies use portal servers, and many use virtual directory software, identity managers and access managers as part of the architecture. Also, not all companies utilize AD as the entry point for sign-on, and there is an XML standard called security assertion markup language (SAML) that supports single sign-on (SSO) within the enterprise, as well as cross enterprises.

Chapter 7—Summary

This chapter described how network architecture evolved from many standards into a single standard based on TCP/IP. It then defined four different network types including internal networks, the Internet, wireless networks, and payment networks. It provided an example of how multiple network types can be combined into a single view supporting the creation of new products and services. The chapter closed with a high-level description of information security and how directory architecture supports the security model for the enterprise.

The following chapter describes various hardware platforms and organizes them into categories based on their unique capabilities. It provides a methodology for selecting the best platform for particular computing requirements and describes how Enterprise Architecture works with other teams to develop the platform architecture.

CHAPTER 8

Platform Architecture

Finally, for those of you interested in the heart of technology, we address the hardware. Computing changed dramatically with the invention of the integrated circuit (IC) at Fairchild Semiconductor in 1961. The IC led to Moore's Law, developed by Gordon Moore in 1965. Gordon Moore stated that the number of circuits on a piece of silicon can double in density about every 18 months. This "law" held true until about the year 2003, when the amount of IC's on a piece of silicon started to generate a disproportionate amount of heat.

Engineers saw the amount of heat generated by the circuits rise at an increasing rate, as more were added. Since 2003, new tricks were introduced to the process of building processors called "multi-core" technology. Multi-core solutions effectively put more than one processor on a piece of silicon to increase capacity, but technically, the scalability of a *single* processor seems to have reached its zenith.

Companies like IBM and Intel are experimenting with new ways to build miniature computers called nanoprocessors. For example, IBM has shown that it can arrange individual atoms into various shapes. In the future, an IC could be as small as a few atoms aligned to perform a task. It remains to be seen, will Moore's Law hold true again? Due to Moore's Law and other factors, the computer industry has evolved extensively since the 1960s into what has become a worldwide explosion of computing power.

As this evolution progressed, companies dedicated to the development, sale, and marketing of computer technology have come and gone, but in their wake is an array of options to choose from. This array of innovative platforms presents a new dilemma for computing professionals. Which computer platform is the best solution for the specific tasks at hand? Even the most expensive system will do a poor job of meeting business requirements if misapplied. This chapter provides the reader with methodologies for selecting the right platform for the computing job.

Types of Platforms

This chapter focuses on the basic processing models used in business, and how each processing model best matches with a type of computing platform. Notice the use of the term *platform* rather than computer. A computer alone will not provide what is needed to process a business transaction. A platform is the combination of an operating system (O/S) matched with the correct processing hardware to meet the needs of the business. The Enterprise Architecture team and various engineering teams within the enterprise make sure that the most cost-effective platforms are employed to meet a business need. The teams work together to assure that systems are purchased and implemented according to a plan which balances cost with capacity and performance. This is accomplished by matching the type of platform to the job required. Platforms can be categorized in to the following major types:

Uniprocessing—A single processor running one physical instance of the O/S with dedicated memory and input/output (I/O) channels. Uniprocessors are the most common type of platform because they are inexpensive, use little power, and require no special environmental support systems (power supply and cooling equipment). Embedded systems in all kinds of consumer and commercial products usually contain uniprocessors. Many PCs are based on a single central processing unit (CPU). However, PCs also usually contain many other uniprocessors to manage tasks offloaded from the main CPU.

Multiprocessing—Multiple CPUs on a single board that run one physical instance of the O/S. The term "board" refers to the circuit board within the computer. It houses the CPU and memory, among other technical components that make up a computer. The O/S in this case is capable of using many CPUs to process work. A multiprocessor platform can access large amounts of contiguous memory (directly attached to the CPUs) and typically has multiple I/O channels. The number of physical CPUs on a single board is usually two or four. Multiprocessor platforms may not require special environmental support and have been implemented in stackable racks or in a common chassis as "blades."

Symmetric multiprocessing (SMP)—Multiple boards with multiple CPUs per board, all running the same logical instance of the O/S. SMP-based systems can access vast amounts of logical memory (indirectly attached memory). SMP-based systems also have many I/O channels. They can scale up to 128 physical CPUs within single backplane architecture. The "backplane" acts like the central nervous system of the computer. All boards containing CPUs are attached to the backplane. SMP-based platforms can be rack mounted (e.g., in four, eight, and sixteen CPU versions in a single unit) or can be floor standing systems (beyond sixteen CPUs up to 128) and usually require special power and cooling environmental support. The number of physical processors and memory available in a typical SMP architecture is a function of the capabilities of the O/S (e.g., thirty-two bit O/S versus sixty-four bit O/S), and what extensions have been made to the O/S to support large systems.

Mainframe computing—Mainframe systems are technically SMPs as they are made up of multiple boards with multiple CPUs per board sharing common backplane architecture. Mainframes employ the same concepts of SMPs with logical contiguous memory, multiple I/O channels, and require specialized environmental support.

Massively parallel processing (MPP)—Multiple boards with multiple CPUs per board using a high bandwidth interconnect between backplanes or boards. An "interconnect" is a high speed network residing within the MPP's architecture which connects boards and/or backplanes into a single logical computing entity. Multiple physical instances of the O/S are loaded within CPUs on boards, and each board has its own memory and I/O channels. Application software running on top of the O/S instances make the system appear as if it were running a single instance of the O/S. Software running on top of the O/S also makes the memory associated with each CPU/board logically contiguous. MPPs are noted for the ability to scale to the thousands of processors. The largest super computers available use MPP architecture. MPPs require special power and cooling environmental support.

Grid computing (grid)—Dissimilar platforms running separately from one another. Work is distributed across various platforms by software designed to manage and move work to the computers with the most available capacity. Memory and I/O across the "grid" are not managed as a single entity. Various operating systems (e.g. UNIX, Windows, Linux) can be used across the computing grid. However, to be considered a grid, each computer must be "grid aware" by running grid software. Grid software makes each system appear as part of a common network of computing power. Technically, grids are really many different platforms and can be composed of any computer type. Usually, grids are composed of lower cost systems like PCs that do not require specialized environmental support.

Table 6 summarizes the various types of platforms available for business use, identifies the typical matching operating systems, and offers positive and negative characteristics of each.

Platform Type	Typical O/S	Positive Aspects	Negative Aspects	Best Use
Uni-Processor	Linux, Palm O/S, RIM Blackberry, Symbian, Windows Mobile, Windows (various)	Inexpensive, dedicated tasks, ubiquitous, low complexity, low power consumption, no special environmental support required	Limited through-put, limited multi-user/application support, very limited I/O channel capability	Dedicated applications, embedded systems, personal and mobile computing.
Multi-Processor	Linux, Windows (various), UNIX (AIX, Solaris, HP-UX),	Inexpensive, multi-tasking, higher through-put than uni-processor, low power and no special environmental support required	Limited scalability limited I/O channel capability	Desktop applications, low-end back-office applications, low-end transaction processing, low-end database applications.
Symmetric Multi-Processor	Linux, Windows (server side), UNIX (All variations)	Moderately expensive, simple to expand to very high levels of processing power, higher through-put, higher transaction processing volume, large memory footprint, larger I/O channel capability	Limited to single-frame scalability. Higher cost and may require specialized environmental support (e.g. power and cooling). Under used capacity is common due to poor capacity planning.	Almost any type of transaction or database processing. Systems can be clustered to break scaling barriers associated with single back-plane architectures.
Massively Parallel Processor	UNIX (usually extended version or modified version of Linux)	Maximum scalability almost no limits, highest through-put, largest memory available, highest transaction processing volume	Very expensive, complex infrastructure, I/O channel and memory need to match CPU power available through the system, requires special environmental support	Large, data intensive applications that do not require coordination of database updates (unless a special RDBMS and/or O/S is used).
Grid Computing	Any but must run grid application to make system "grid-aware". Grid application could be O/S dependent	Inexpensive, utilizes unused capacity on various platforms	Difficult to coordinate data updates within disparate platforms.	Workloads that do not require coordination of database updates or updates can be synchronized at a later time frame then when presented.
Mainframe Computing	z OS, MVS, Linux, TPF	Highly scalable centralized platform known for superior memory access and I/O channel capabilities	Usually requires expensive application software to obtain high through-put and transaction processing capabilities (e.g. CICS or other)	Centralized I/O bound workloads. On-line processing requiring the highest level of data integrity from a centralized location.

Table 6—Platform Types

Some of these platform types have overlapping characteristics. Presented in the table are the predominant characteristics and suggested uses for the specific type of computing platform. Understanding platforms organized in this manner is necessary for establishing a methodology for platform selection for the company.

Scale-Up vs. Scale-Out

The classic dilemma for any enterprise architect is whether to use an array of inexpensive systems (scale-out) or a single large platform (scale-up) to meet the needs of the business. While there is considerable overlap between the two styles of processing, there is a methodology that can help determine the best mix of computing power for the set of applications required to run on the hardware. The following figure summarizes the major considerations involved in platform selection.

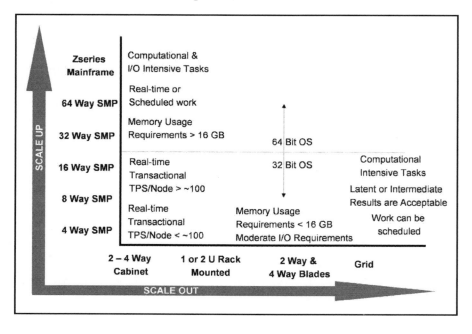

Figure 20—Platform Selection Criteria

As figure 20 shows, the main considerations include the rate of transaction processing required, measured in transactions per second (TPS), and the amount of memory needed by the applications. The scale-out architecture will support high volumes of TPS, but if the application also needs access to over 16GB of random access memory (RAM), then a scale-up solution is better. A third major consideration also comes into play: the rate of I/O needed to meet application requirements. The combination of all three—TPS, memory access, and I/O intensity, drives the decision toward one end of the scale or the other.

A grid-enabled architecture (which is the extreme example of scale-out) can support almost limitless amounts of TPS, but if the applications running on the grid-aware systems need to access memory across the grid, transaction latency will be introduced (because, by definition, the other systems are across a network). Also, if the results of processing must be available in real time across the grid, more latency will be introduced as the database management engine synchronizes data updates made to local storage attached to the grid-enabled systems.

On the other end of the spectrum, if applications require real-time access to large amounts of memory (over 16GB) and/or share results of I/O operations on a transaction-by-transaction basis, then an SMP architecture (scale-up) works best. SMPs support access to large amounts of memory without crossing a data network external to the computer. Therefore, up to certain limits, many CPUs using large amounts of memory can be used together as a single system without network latency.

Keeping the system in balance is the key consideration when matching a platform to computing requirements. Platform architecture must be in balance when designed and remain in balance over time, to run efficiently. Striking a balance between TPS, memory utilization and I/O is difficult but must be done to maximize hardware investments. Even a single image SMP or mainframe-based application that performs too much I/O in relation to TPS processing (or computational work) will not perform at its best. Figure 20 is meant to act as a guideline and is by no means precise. Systems engineers and platform architects need an understanding of application requirements to design the best platform.

In a perfect world, systems engineers will have a solid set of usage requirements in hand before they design the processing platform. However, in reality, funding for projects is usually obtained at the start of the project life cycle when the application has not even been designed or purchased yet. This situation is quite normal. However, it is possible to obtain the correct platform design, with cost estimates up front, by following this guideline:

> *The best approach is to default toward scale-up (SMP) and only place solutions on scale-out that do not require data synchronization in real-time across computing nodes.*

SMP architectures are more forgiving than scale-out architectures because it is easier to size an SMP and make up for having imperfect information at the start of a new project. If an SMP is undersized, additional processing power and memory can be added without redesigning the whole platform architecture.

Conversely, placing a system that is heavily I/O bound, with transaction results that are needed immediately, on a scale-out design is more risky. This is due to the potential for adding transaction latency as work spreads out across the grid (or blade chassis). So applications that are similar to batch processing, where results do not need to be aggregated immediately, or that have no requirements to manage transaction integrity across systems, can be easily placed onto scale-out architectures.

Blade servers are often used to host web servers. By default, a web server does not maintain transaction integrity, and the state of a user session can be reassigned on a next-request-in basis. Web servers use http as their communication protocol, and therefore, being stateless, the workload can easily be spread across an array of servers without negatively impacting data integrity or system performance.

Now imagine a different application, such as handling airline reservations from a call center. Each phone call results in many transactions that must be reflected in the database immediately. Systems that process unplanned levels of transactions (variable call volumes) and need to retain data integrity immediately upon the user hitting "enter", cannot be run easily on scale-out architectures. Using scale-out architecture for these requires expensive transaction management technology to assure data integrity. Usually, the cost of adding transaction management software and data synchronization technology outweigh the cost savings of the scale-out design. In these cases, from a TCO perspective, using a scale-up design is the better choice.

Virtual Platforms

Just to make matters more complicated, a platform strategy includes using virtual machines (VMs). Virtual machines appear as if they are separate computers running on the same physical hardware. They are renditions of the operating system that are created by software as extrapolations of the underlying O/S. Some hardware vendors have combined virtualization into their firmware and hardware architecture, making virtualization not only a result of software but of a combination of specialized hardware and software. Firmware is a term used to describe a combination of software and hardware circuit design providing basic services in a computer's architecture. Some computer manufacturers have created virtual CPUs through the combination of software and circuits designed to run program instructions.

Platform virtualization is one of the most important innovations of I/T. There have been virtualized operating systems around since the 1970s, but virtualization has recently become one of the most important elements of platform architecture. By creating virtual instances of an operating system, more applications can be run on a single hardware component. Running multiple applications on a single server creates greater computing density within the company's data center. Increasing computing density lowers the TCO of computing at the enterprise level. Companies have completed massive server consolidation projects which, in part, were enabled through the use of virtualization.

Virtualization takes place at the lowest levels of the systems architecture. Computer chip manufactures like IBM and Intel have developed "multicore" architectures. Depending on the manufacturer, the operating system running on top of the multicore design may or may not be aware of how many logical processors are available at any point in time. For example, a multicore Intel Chip typically is loaded with the Windows operating system or possibly one of the variations of Linux. Neither Windows 2000 nor Linux supports the ability to define "virtual engines" at the O/S level. It is true that systems may run faster due to the multicore architecture underneath the O/S. However, since Windows 2000 and Linux do not natively support "logical O/S partitioning," work cannot be predetermined for specific logical processors.

Companies like IBM, Sun Microsystems, and HP have developed UNIX-based operating systems that allow systems administrators to set up logical partitions (LPARs) within the system architecture. LPARs provide the ability to dedicate portions of the CPU, memory, and I/O to applications and assure that there is no interference from other LPARs running on the same platform. Each vendor has designed their LPAR capabilities differently, and there are pros and cons of each solution. IBM supports both static and dynamic LPARs in their AIX operating system. Sun Microsystems and HP each support static LPARs (partitions) in Solaris and HP-UX respectively. Using dynamic LPARs, the system can reassign work based on parameters set by the systems administrator while the system is running. To reset parameters in a static LPAR-based system, the server must be shut down and restarted by the systems administrator.

Windows 2000 and Linux do not support logical partitioning, which created a market opportunity for some vendors. For example, EMC^2 owns a company called VMWare Inc. which markets software called VMWare. VMWare provides the virtualization layer of software for Intel processor architectures. With VMWare, companies can establish virtual copies of Windows or Linux on a single CPU. Depending on the scalability factors described earlier, when using VMWare, it is common to obtain more than ten virtual O/S instances on a single two-CPU Intel-based server. In some cases, the ratio can be as high as 15 virtual CPUs to one physical CPU, but that depends on the factors described in "Scale-up vs. Scale-Out".

Using products like VMWare and LPARs, system administrators can drive up the utilization of hardware platforms. This reduces the actual number of physical servers needed to meet the needs of the business, using less floor space in the data center and requiring less environmental support. All this saves money and reduces the total cost of computing at the enterprise level.

Another form of virtualization is hosting applications designed for the personal computer, or other remote computers, within sessions running within a single physical server. Citrix Systems Inc. markets technology allowing PC users to run desktop applications within sessions on servers over a network. The software creates virtual desktop O/S images on servers.

The technology employs a Citrix Client installed on a users PC. The client communicates with a Citrix Presentation Server over a network, where individual user sessions are managed. While technically, this is not virtualization of the server operating system, it does drive up server utilization numbers from a data center perspective. Citrix is used when users are remote from their offices and need access to a virtual workspace composed of what was normally running on their desktop computer. Companies are also using this technology to provide access to internally developed and purchased applications without the need to deploy desktop software external to the enterprise.

However, just as in the case with operating system virtualization, the ratio of user sessions per single instance of Citrix Presentation Server is a key consideration. As the ratio of sessions to servers increases, overall performance will decrease. Balancing PC like response time, with how many sessions are supported per server, is the critical success factor for Citrix. The number of PC sessions per Citrix Presentation Server is the key factor in determining the cost-effectiveness of a remote session solution.

Citrix Systems Inc. is also focused on the O/S virtualization market and announced the acquisition of XenSource in the summer of 2007. XenSource which supports both virtual Windows and virtual Linux, was a major competitor to VMWare, so it appears that companies will have more choices when it comes to virtualization in the coming years.

Designing for High Availability

Keeping systems available and meeting user expectations are probably at the top of most I/T managers' priority lists. Like the balance required in platform selection, managing the balance between cost (investment) and availability is important. Computer systems can be failure proof, but achieving higher availability means higher systems costs. Therefore, Enterprise Architecture and Systems Engineering together must strike the appropriate balance between cost and system availability.

As is the case for platform selection, designing for high availability starts with the basic business requirements. Applications can be categorized by their level of criticality to the business functions they support. Below are examples of how most companies categorize availability. All of the categories assume that systems are allowed to be taken out of use for three hours per week for maintenance reasons. Outages that occur outside of the planned down period would be considered a systems failure.

Crit. Level 1—available 99.999 percent or more

> Level 1 criticality means that the system cannot be down for more than about 5 minutes over the course of an entire year. The calculation is usually done by taking the total hours in a year (8,760), subtracting out any planned/scheduled downtime (approximately three hours/week for example), converting hours into minutes and multiplying by .00001.

Crit. Level 2—available 99.99 percent or more

Level 2 criticality means that the system cannot be down for more than about 52 minutes over the course of an entire year. The multiplier in this scenario is .0001.

Crit. Level 3—available 99.9 percent or more

Level 3 criticality means that the system cannot be down for more than about 8.6 hours over the course of the entire year. The multiplier in this case is .001.

There are two other dimensions worth noting regarding availability. These are *recovery time objective* (RTO) and *recovery point objective* (RPO). RTO is the time that the business can wait until the application is available following an outage. It is the time allowed to bring the system back online once a major failure has occurred.

RPO references the currency (or freshness) of the data available once the system has been restored to working order. For example, if it takes one hour to restore the system (RTO), in what state is the data when the systems comes back online? Is the data one hour old, or is it up to date from when the outage first occurred? Using this example, if one hour old information is acceptable when the system is restored, then the RTO is equal to the RPO. Assuming the same example, if data must be current as of the last five minutes when the system is restored, then the RTO is one hour and the RPO is five minutes.

The platform architecture required for systems with very short recovery time objectives is much different from those with longer recovery time objectives. The combination of the *recovery time* and *recovery point* objectives will have a major impact on the platform architecture chosen for the applications running on them. Figure 21 shows the relationship between the platform architecture and recovery objectives. Crit. Level 1 applications fall into the lower left corner of the chart. Crit. Level 2 applications fall in the middle, followed by Crit. Level 3, in the upper right corner.

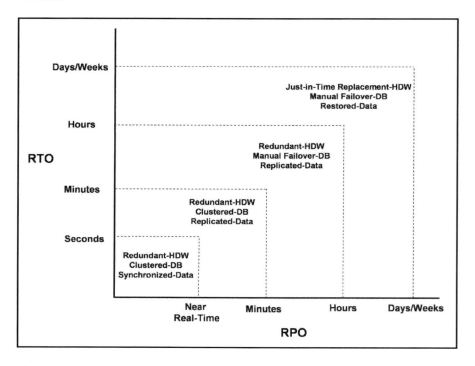

Figure 21—Availability Model

Figure 21 shows the different platform architectures required to meet the availability requirements of applications organized by level of criticality.

Users of Crit. 1 applications would not be aware there was a system outage because backup systems take over processing without delay and without losing data integrity. These applications require redundant hardware that is clustered, supporting automatic fail-over capabilities. Data on each redundant system must be synchronized across all platforms. These redundant systems are sometimes called "active-active" as they work in tandem to assure zero data loss and zero impact to users if failures occur. They also tend to be the most expensive to implement and are complicated to manage.

Crit. 2 applications can be recovered in minutes. They require almost the same investment in redundant hardware as the Crit. 1 category. Due to the short time to recover (minutes), redundant systems are usually synchronized on a transaction-by-transaction basis. Redundant systems can run in "active-active" mode or "active-passive" mode and still meet Crit. 2 availability requirements.

Data in "active-passive" architecture is synchronized between the primary system and backup system on a periodic basis. To meet Crit. 2 availability requirements, the "passive" system receives updates from the primary system within seconds of the primary completing its work. Users may need to log-on again to reach the passive system in the event of an unplanned outage of the primary. They expect data on the backup system to be current to the last update performed on the primary system, before the outage occurred.

Crit. 3 applications utilize less expensive and less complicated redundant system architecture. In the event of a major failure, processing is automatically or manually moved from one platform to another. Since the time to recover is longer than Crit.1 and Crit. 2, redundant systems can be synchronized on a periodic basis. Crit. 3 availability requirements are also met with "active-passive" architecture. The "active-passive" architecture supports data synchronization using point-in-time copies or system log files.

By positioning applications into the Crit. 3 category, management is agreeing that data loss is a possibility in the event of an extended unplanned outage. Applications assigned this level of availability may be unusable for hours or days. Typically, management accepts the lower level of availability because the application may not be the system-of-record. It may receive input from other systems that are managed at a higher level of criticality, making it recoverable over the long-term. Many decision support systems are managed in this manner, as they are important, but the business can continue operations without them. For these,

data can be restored from backup files and brought up to date
using files containing updates that occurred in other systems
during the outage period.

Storage Architecture

Just as there are numerous choices available regarding platforms,
there are many options available for data storage. Storage costs have
declined dramatically over the last ten years. It is very common
today to talk in terms of terabytes of data when, just a few years
ago, almost everyone referred to data in terms of gigabytes. Storage
technology has not only evolved in terms of density (amount of
data saved) but in performance (access time to data).

Storage vendors such as EMC^2, IBM, and Hitachi have invested
heavily in software products to improve on data density and
data access time. While these vendors were busy working on
improving their primary storage products, other vendors saw a
new market for low cost, high volume storage solutions. Vendors
such as NetApp and 3PAR took low-cost storage devices normally
used in PCs and file servers, and placed them into storage arrays.
The new storage architecture addressed requirements to store
ever-larger amounts of data at reduced costs.

As these new storage vendors prospered, the major
manufactures also began offering multiple products aimed at
different price and service points for their customers. Competition
between vendors led to storage solutions organized into four
distinct tiers. These range from the highest speed medium density
(tier-1) to slower speed higher density (tier-2), to lowest speed
and highest density (tier-3). The fourth tier is magnetic tape. Tape
is still needed for the long-term backup and disaster recovery
requirements of the enterprise.

Engineers must match the computing platform with the
appropriate storage architecture to optimize cost, performance,
and availability. Applications that process high volumes of
transactions (I/O intense) need the lowest response times.
Therefore, these need the fastest and most expensive tier-1
storage solutions. Applications that tend to process transactions

intermittently, or do not have strict service level requirements, may utilize less costly tier-2 storage. Applications that only access information periodically to meet audit or historical reporting requirements can use the least-expensive tier 3 storage.

Storage units in all three tiers can be accessed through network architecture. A *storage area network* (SAN) is used to organize and manage disk units (each unit contains many drives arranged in arrays). A SAN is architected with fiber-optic cable and *san-switches* providing the fastest access times possible. The architecture supports breaking vast amounts of storage devices into independent *areas*. Changes to storage layouts within areas are independent of other areas and can be performed from a common administrative console. Storage areas improve flexibility by making adding and changing storage allocations simpler, requiring less engineering labor.

Storage can also be managed using different network architecture than SAN. Servers can be connected to storage units directly thought network-attached storage (NAS). NAS provides the same high-speed access to disk units (and the arrays of disks within them), but costs less to implement. Since there is not a hierarchy of storage units in NAS, there is not a need for SAN switches. Rather, a UNIX server acts as a "NAS head" and controls access to all storage units on behalf of the servers needing access to the disk drives. Since the NAS head acts as the controller for other servers in the network, there is no costly software required on each server and no need for costly SAN switches in the architecture.

The trade off between NAS and SAN is hardware/software cost versus labor costs. NAS requires less hardware and software, therefore is less expensive. However, since NAS is connected directly to servers, moving devices and adding storage takes more effort than would be required using a SAN. If there are many changes required to NAS, more engineers will be required to keep up with project demand. SANs are networks of storage devices requiring more hardware and software. However, these are managed by *area* from a single management console. By isolating changes to areas, the amount of labor required to keep up with changes is reduced. While it may seem less expensive to use a NAS, if there are many changes expected to the storage architecture at a frequent rate, then SAN will cost less in the long run.

Chapter 8—Summary

This chapter described the fundamentals of platform selection. It began by describing various types of computing technology and prescribed a method to select the correct hardware and operating system configuration to meet the requirements of the business. It discussed the importance of maintaining a balance in computing power stated as TPS, memory access and I/O. Virtualization was discussed as a method to drive up computing density and drive down TCO. A model was presented describing the trade-offs between making systems highly available and cost effective. Meeting application availability requirements was described as a matching process between platform architecture and availability objectives set by the business. The chapter closed with an introduction to storage systems architecture.

Keeping systems up and running is the theme of Chapter 9, "Operations Management Architecture". It introduces systems management and some of the key technologies used to control the I/T operating environment within the enterprise.

CHAPTER 9

Operations Management Architecture

At an elemental level, if systems within the enterprise are not reliable, nothing else really matters. It is just a fact that systems architecture is complicated. While the goal of systems architecture is to make things *appear* to be simple, technology is complex. The best designs and business solutions will fail if they are routinely unavailable, perform poorly, or cause business processes to fail. Therefore, management of each layer of the architecture, namely applications, information, networks, and platforms requires discipline and a set of management systems aimed at "keeping the lights on." This chapter describes the basic functions of operations management and identifies the key components needed to provide the business with reliable performance on a day-to-day basis.

Operations Building Blocks

Operating the complex labyrinth of technologies that make up today's enterprise is a tall task, and to assure the business stays healthy without using large numbers of human resources requires an investment in an operating infrastructure. The basic building blocks of operations management have evolved over the years to include the following major functions:

- problem management
- change management

- asset management
- configuration management
- capacity management

The enterprise must invest in each of these functions, albeit with varying degrees of automation; otherwise, the result will be poor systems availability leading to lost revenues in the long run.

The most basic function of operations management is *problem management*. Problem management is the process of identifying systems problems, recording events, conducting problem-determination tasks, performing problem prioritization, and overseeing problem resolution. Most companies have instituted a structure for ranking problems to help management prioritize problems as they are reported. Problems are typically classified by the impact they have on business operations, the number of customers, business users and suppliers affected, and the level of impact to daily business operations.

Problem priorities are usually stated in terms of their severity level which is reflective of the impact on business operations. Problems with a severity level of 1 (SEV1) are those which manifest themselves with a major impact on business operations. For example, a SEV1 problem means that a system that generates revenue, serves customers/suppliers, or maintains the safety of individuals is not operating. Usually, staff assigned to work on SEV1 problems work nonstop until either a mitigating solution is running, or the problem has been resolved.

Severity level 2 (SEV2) usually means that some business processes are unavailable, but there will be no revenue loss, customer/supplier impact, or unsafe conditions. SEV2 problems still need to be resolved quickly, but since critical business operations are able to continue, more time can be taken in the resolution process. The time allowed by management to resolve SEV2 problems varies by company, but normally is not more than a few hours at most.

Management considers problems classified as severity level 3 (SEV3) to be a nuisance for business operations. SEV3 problems do not need to be resolved in a short time period. However, no more than a few days of impact are allowed by management.

While it is possible to record and prioritize problems manually, a problem management system is normally used to make the process run smoothly. These systems use what is called a "problem ticket" to record and track reported events. Problem management application software can receive information about problems in the form of system-generated events using the simple network management protocol (SNMP). This protocol is supported by almost all technology vendors today and is a standard way for networks and computers to post events about what is happening while they are running or when they begin to fail.

People can also report problems in addition to those reported systematically. An application user can call the help desk and report an event. The help desk worker then uses the online version of the problem management application to generate a problem ticket. Problem management systems support both automated and manual escalation processes. For example, if hundreds of users call the help desk about an application failure, a problem classified as a SEV2 priority can be automatically escalated to a SEV1 level.

Problem tickets are records on a database and since they are assigned a unique identifier, can be tracked from the problem determination stage through the problem resolution stage. In addition, ticket information from the database can be analyzed to either help prevent problems or reduce resolution time for recurring problems. Management metrics can be generated by using data from the problem management system. These metrics can also be used to support initiatives that eliminate or reduce the quantity, duration and severity (impact) of systems problems.

The next major building block of operations management is *change management*. Change management consists of a set of procedures designed to work with a change management system. Procedures are defined by operations management personnel working with others across I/T. Change management procedures are agreements about when and how changes can be introduced to production systems.

There is usually a direct relationship between the amount of change allowed in the environment and the availability/stability of business systems. In most companies, as the quantity of change requests increases, the number of problem tickets also increases. Therefore, controls are placed on who can request a change, who can implement a change, how often a change can be made, and to which systems. Typically, a *change calendar* is developed that shows which I/T teams are requesting changes to their systems over what time frame. The change calendar can be analyzed by the operations management staff to look for overlaps or conflicts between systems impacted by changes.

Having a comprehensive list of applications and the infrastructure components they rely on is also a critical success factor of any good change management process or system. Enterprise architecture plays a major role in maintaining the overall application architecture along with a view of the technology stack required by applications. In an advanced state, enterprise architecture maintains the *enterprise architecture repository* which documents applications and technical architectures across the enterprise. The repository provides valuable input to operations management, as staff looks for cross-system impacts before changes are actually implemented.

Although not technically part of the operations management function, *asset management* is also a key building block of operations management. As hardware and software is purchased, information about these company assets must be recorded. Usually, asset management is a function of the company's accounting department. Because most technology can be capitalized and depreciated, each technical component must be uniquely identified along with the date of acquisition, date of installation, cost basis, and estimated useful life.

Asset information can be used by operations management for a clear view of the technical components in use across the enterprise, as well as for project planning purposes. Whether equipment is leased or purchased, plans for replacement can be developed by analyzing the information in the asset management system. Data from the asset management database can be linked to, or loaded into, the enterprise architecture repository by the enterprise architecture department. Asset IDs can be used as keys into the overall view of technology in use across the business, and this information is valuable to operations management staff engaged in problem determination, impact analysis, and problem-resolution activities.

Enterprise architecture is the custodian of the total view of the company's technology matrix. Obtaining a comprehensive technology view requires asset information to be loaded into the enterprise architecture repository. The enterprise architecture repository typically does not contain all the details needed by asset planners or operations personnel. Therefore, only a subset of information about technology assets need be stored in the repository. Enterprise architecture is focused on assuring that technical standards are followed as new technology is introduced across the company. They use high level technical information to make long term plans regarding the overall technology configuration of the company.

In contrast, operations management needs information at a detailed level to assist with problem and change management activities. Capturing and maintaining the detailed view of technology used across the company is called, *configuration management*. The configuration management processes within operations management rely on a *configuration management database* (CMDB). The CMDB either receives real-time updates from the asset management system or, at a minimum, is synchronized with it on a periodic basis.

Operations management utilizes the CMDB in root-cause analysis regarding problems. The best CMDB systems support an automated discovery capability. The CMDB system can automatically discover hardware and software after installation on the company's network. The information obtained from the automated discovery process is matched with information obtained from asset management, creating a comprehensive view into computer and network operations.

Since the CMDB contains the most detailed view of technology in the company, its information can be uploaded to the enterprise architecture repository. The following figure shows how each of these sources of technical data forms a complete picture of the technology within the company.

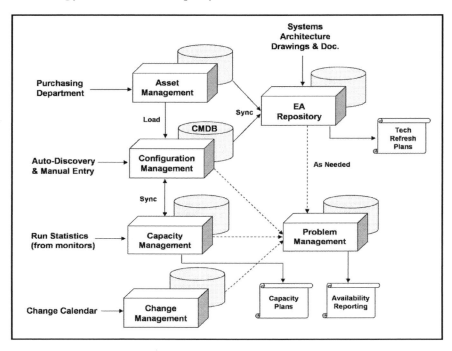

Figure 22—Operations Management Systems Architecture

Businesses want to get the most out of their technology investments. To accomplish this goal, operations management is responsible for running systems as close as possible to maximum capacity, without degrading performance. In order for operations management to assure that systems perform as needed, they need information about utilization. *Capacity management* is an activity that uses data obtained from performance management systems that monitor utilization.

Typically, it is expensive to capture detailed run-time statistics on every system across the enterprise. Therefore, most performance management systems take snapshots of system utilization statistics on a periodic basis. Operations management personnel determine which platforms are most critical and at which times during the processing day these snapshots should be taken. Data derived from the monitors is loaded into a database where analysis can be performed. Detailed graphs show the level of CPU utilization and the amount of free memory available on servers. Other graphs show the amount of free storage available on disk units within the data centers.

Some monitors are installed to measure server utilization and storage availability. Other monitors are installed on network components to measure network bandwidth utilization. The capacity management team merges utilization reports across servers, networks, and storage systems. They use this information to develop trend reports that highlight areas of potential problems. The capacity plan developed by the capacity management team is used to ward off problems that may arise due to capacity issues. Performance analysis reports are also used to plan hardware upgrades, network bandwidth upgrades, and the addition of storage to the pool of available disk space.

Standard Operating Procedures

Operations management systems work as a unit to help I/T deliver reliable systems that run the business. Since these systems work in a mode where they cannot be seen or experienced by business personnel, justifying the investment to purchase or develop them can be difficult. Control procedures are needed whether a company invests in packaged applications or mainly uses manual labor. However, it makes sense to use packaged software solutions in this area because in the long run, it is less expensive than using people to run manual procedures.

Building a cost/benefit case for these "invisible investments" is difficult. Therefore, I/T leadership must work to convince upper management that these investments are necessary and required. They are a cost of doing business in today's technology-driven world. To justify investments in infrastructure, many companies are using industry wide best practice as their leading argument. Since the year 2000, companies have worked together to establish a set of best practices that can be used to run I/T operations. One most notable set of standards is the Information Technology Infrastructure Library (ITIL).

The concept of ITIL is based on treating operations management like a company that is in the business of servicing systems. By treating operations management functions as if they were services offered by a company, I/T will standardize the day-to-day activities needed to maintain system stability. Through standardization, I/T can make the case to upper management that these services are used by all mature companies, and they are a necessity, not a luxury.

Since ITIL is based on standards established by ISO/IEC, the standards are known worldwide, and no single entity can control their evolution. ITIL is composed of five publications: service strategy, service design, service transition, service operation, and continuous service improvement. These five publications are updated as best practices are added. More information can be found about them by consulting the web site, *www.itil-itsm-world. com.*

Not all companies have embraced ITIL, but every company that has a large investment in systems uses the basic building blocks of operations management to manage their environment. Once a company has invested in these functions, it would be wise to adopt at least some of the best practices and standards offered by ITIL. For over thirty years, companies defined their own systems management policies, procedures, and standards. Although I/T can support the business without standards from outsiders, why not take advantage of the best efforts of others in the industry? A close look at what ITIL has to offer can lead to real improvements within the operations management function within the company.

EA and Operations Management

The enterprise architecture function does not normally play a daily role in running I/T operations. However, enterprise architecture can be of great assistance in establishing and maintaining the standards associated with operations management. Enterprise architecture maintains the global technical view across the company through the enterprise architecture repository. This technical repository provides major benefits to the operations personnel, as they work on daily problems or make plans for future technical changes. Enterprise architecture assists with technology planning activities conducted by operations management. The two departments work together to request funding from upper management for infrastructure investments. Both departments lend support to each other as they work to manage the total cost of ownership (TCO) of the technology.

Chapter 9—Summary

This chapter presented an overview of the operations management function within the enterprise. As first described in chapter 4, operations management provides the underpinnings to all other components of the enterprise architecture framework.

This chapter described the building blocks of operations management. These are problem management, change management, asset management, configuration management, and capacity planning. An overview of each of these was presented along with a systems architecture diagram. The chapter introduced a relatively new set of best practices called ITIL, and described the importance of adopting industry best practices regarding I/T systems management. The chapter concluded with comments about how the enterprise architecture function complements operations management.

This chapter concludes the series of chapters devoted to describing the enterprise architecture framework. Chapter 4 introduced the framework, and chapters 5-9 describe its major components. These components included application architecture, information architecture, network architecture, platform architecture, and operations management architecture.

The final chapters cover service-oriented architecture, managing the architecture department and the evolution of the function.

Chapter 10

Service-Oriented Architecture

One of the best developments affecting enterprise architecture is the popularization of *service-oriented architecture* (SOA). This design discipline has been covered in the press, described in magazines, and popularized for non I/T professionals. SOA has focused the spotlight on technical systems architecture and how the enterprise architecture function can become a strategic resource for companies.

However, with this notoriety comes the responsibility of carrying through on what SOA promises. Otherwise, it will be viewed as just another over hyped technology that promises the impossible. Since SOA is so important to the credibility of enterprise architecture, this chapter is devoted to the topic. The chapter offers a definition of SOA and differentiates SOA strategy from SOA technology. It describes the major components and standards of SOA, and how SOA is likely to evolve.

SOA Background

Like anything that is heavily promoted by the media, various people apply whatever definition or meaning they believe to be true to describe the phenomenon. This has been no different with SOA.

A simple but relevant definition for SOA is:

> *A service-oriented architecture is a software design discipline that leverages open standards to provide reusable services matching the business model of the company.*

This definition is appropriate because of the emphasis placed on matching services to the business model. Many have defined SOA as any component of software that has been enabled with the extensible markup language (XML) or software components enabled with a Web-service interface. (A Web-service interface is one that follows standards developed by the W3C called, "WS-standards"). While these technologies enable SOA, they, alone, do not add significant value to the business. The most valuable aspect of SOA, as explained later, is that the systems architecture can affect the business model of a company.

SOA, as a concept, is not new to I/T. The service concept has evolved from earlier work focused on the development of reusable software. Object oriented programming (OOP) emerged in the late 1980s. Many of the concepts introduced by OOP have been incorporated into SOA. In the mid-1990s, the Object Management Group (OMG) developed the common object request broker architecture (CORBA). CORBA is based on a software design discipline in which software objects run decoupled from one another, as long as all parties agree to a common interface standard called the interface definition language (IDL).

The theory behind CORBA is that software can interoperate through a standard interface definition based on common standards set by an independent standards body. Technical details inside the servicing object are hidden from the consumer object. CORBA supports multiple programming language bindings and can run over various network level integration protocols. CORBA gained traction in the development community, but implementations depended on software tools that were proprietary and complicated.

As the Java programming language emerged in the mid-1990s, new remote object integration techniques were introduced. In particular, remote method invocation (RMI), which was easy to implement, gained popularity among software developers. By including an object request broker (ORB) within the baseline Java software libraries, developers could invoke CORBA without even being aware of it. Using RMI, software developers could run Java programs called "beans" loosely coupled from each other, without having to deal with the set of integration tools required by CORBA. Basically, RMI includes the CORBA tooling but its infrastructure is hidden from programmers using RMI.

Whether software objects are developed using CORBA compliant tools or Java/RMI, both alternatives can leverage the internet inter-ORB protocol (IIOP). IIOP provides messaging and transaction delivery services for remote software objects. Java software objects can communicate using RMI over a network using either IIOP or http. Regardless of the messaging protocol, when using RMI, objects must be written in the Java programming language only.

Therefore, a key problem with RMI is that it assumes both ends of a transaction between objects are written in the Java programming language. There are many situations when Java programs cannot be the end point of a transaction, especially when the transaction crosses platforms. Therefore, RMI is not able to bridge non-Java environments without other technology. This issue gave rise to another set of products in the late 1990s called enterprise application integration (EAI) tools.

EAI tools were developed to bridge the cross-platform gap and resolve differences between programming languages, communication protocols, and transaction-state management. EAI vendors helped solve these integration problems, but the technology was costly and usually cumbersome for I/T to utilize. More importantly, companies became dependent on EAI vendors. Companies seeking vendor independence in their application suite found themselves married to a new vendor, namely the EAI vendor. What was needed was a set of open standards that were vendor independent and easy to use. Therefore, EAI saw limited success.

From the 1990s to today, the Internet has dominated software design and deployment. Web-based solutions were created that relied on the stateless nature of http. The fact that web browsers assume a stateless world has been a key driver in the development of software architecture over the past ten years.

XML, which is a derivative of standard generalized markup language (SGML), has gained popularity with software engineers. SGML is a tag language created as an extension to generalized markup language (GML) defined by IBM in the 1960s. GML standardized document organization and formatting rules for word-processing software. SGML used formatting tags and data descriptors to create data semantic schemas. As a derivative of SGML, XML became a popular tool to use for defining data semantics between applications. XML is endorsed by the W3C.

With important companies like Sun Microsystems, Microsoft, and IBM on the W3C, true cross-platform architecture standards emerged. The W3C created new standards including the simple object access protocol (SOAP), web-service definition language (WSDL), universal description, discovery and integration (UDDI), and a host of service definitions typically referred to as the "WS-standards."

Since many of these standards assume transactions are stateless in nature, they solve cross-platform integration issues. Being sponsored by a consortium, they can be adopted by any vendor or enterprise. What makes the "WS-standards" different than those of the 1990s, is that almost all software vendors are using them without modifying them for proprietary purposes. Based on open standards, *Web-services* have become the perfect solution for developing loosely coupled software that can run across a network and across various platforms.

Strategy or Technology

Chapter 2 defined business strategy and put business strategy into a technological context. Three of the four quadrants in the business strategy matrix shown in figure 4 rely on loosely coupled enterprise architecture. SOA represents an opportunity to match I/T infrastructure with the business-operating model of the company. It provides the infrastructure to make the business model work as planned.

Unfortunately, people tend to confuse technology concepts with strategic concepts. Confusing the idea of "web service enabling" software with the strategy of organizing the business into centers of excellence or *service centers,* has created disconnects between business leaders and I/T leaders regarding SOA. The greatest benefits of SOA come from reducing operating costs and improving business flexibility. Costs can be reduced through improving efficiency using centralized business processes and adopting best practices. Flexibility to respond to changing market conditions comes from reusing common services across the company. If this is SOA's objective, then perhaps a better term to describe it is *service-oriented enterprise* (SOE).

The SOE is a company that understands what core processes make it competitive within its market and which processes are commodities. Knowing which functions actually differentiate the company in a crowded market allows management to focus resources (capital and labor) on the things that add the most value. Business functions that support the core business model may need customized software solutions or specialized I/T infrastructure. Other areas are important, but would not garner the same management attention and investment as the core.

By analyzing business processes and separating the "core/strategic" from the "non-core/tactical", management can develop a new organization structure based on services. Business processes running in different segments of the company can be combined to formulate common service functions. For example, if multiple lines of business each have a target marketing function, why not pool the resources and develop a target marketing *service.* This way, different and redundant technology used by each area can be consolidated into a single software suite and target marketing database infrastructure. Figure 23 shows a simple example of consolidation into a service model.

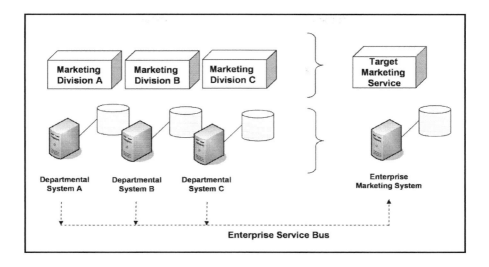

Figure 23—Service Model

In this example, the company is organized into three distinct divisions. Over time, each division has invested in its own target marketing technology in support of each unique set of marketing business processes. Obviously, converging to a set of common processes using a single system will reduce operating costs and improve the effectiveness of the target marketing function.

The difficulty comes, in consolidating the various systems. There are number of issues to be addressed before convergence can be completed. These include understanding the various processes in each division, understanding each system and its data, and developing a convergence plan that does not disrupt normal operations in each division.

A company cannot wait years for transition plans to be completed before adopting a service oriented strategy. The enterprise architecture department can help with transition by defining enterprise-wide integration standards. The integration standards derived from the W3C, are implemented through a common integration "bus". The term "bus", is taken from the computer hardware engineering discipline. Computers have a single high speed network within, that all components connect

151

to, called a "bus". The enterprise service bus (ESB) provides consistent communications architecture to services, similar to the hardware "bus" within servers.

By leveraging the enterprise integration standards deployed via the ESB, a new system can be introduced, while leaving legacy applications in place. Over time, legacy applications can be retired, as the data and processes of each division are collapsed into the new entity.

It is imperative that the older divisional systems be shut off; otherwise, total costs will increase with the addition of the new platform. Companies must carry through with their plans to converge redundant functions, including the business applications. Otherwise, moving to a service-based model will add costs not reduce them. Adding new systems without retiring the legacy causes data redundancy leading to inefficient operating procedures, limiting business model flexibility. Therefore, a multiyear plan, sponsored by senior management, is paramount to the success of moving to the service-oriented enterprise (SOE).

So the *strategy* is to refocus resources in the company to reduce costs, improve business processes, and increase flexibility. The *technology,* on the other hand, is all about applying industry-accepted standards to the software development process. Simply enabling older software with new web-service-based standards does not address the overall strategy. Building reusable software components does have a positive effect on costs, but the business will not experience the major benefits associated with SOA without addressing the strategy.

SOA Technology

While it is true that most benefits from adoption of SOA come from changes in the business-operating model, these changes are almost impossible to achieve without a new underlying infrastructure. Service orientation from a technical perspective means applying the standards set by the W3C to software. To do that, software across the company must be engineered as reusable components. Of course, companies cannot afford to throw out all applications and purchase or rewrite them all at once. Therefore, SOA can really only be adopted according to an evolutionary model.

As the business determines which of its functions are core/ strategic, I/T must also analyze the application portfolio. Using the enterprise architecture repository, lead architects identify the best candidates to be "service enabled." A priority list of the core business functions can be used to target which applications to break into discrete service components.

Once the list of candidate services is agreed upon, the next step is to classify services by business function. For example, a process that assigns customer account numbers would work the same across all lines of business. Since customer account numbers must be unique, there should be no differences in account number generation and assignment logic across the company. A service that does not invoke business rules and is useful regardless of the business context is called a *utility service*.

A business function such as customer billing, is more complicated due to differences in business processes and rules across lines of business. Services that require unique business logic depending on the context in which they are used are called *foundational services*. Foundational services can be reused, but they are designed to support unique business requirements. Lines of business that adopt foundational services also inherit the business rules associated with the service.

If upper management wants all customers to be billed the same way using the same rules, regardless of the line of business, then the customer billing service would be a good candidate as an *enterprise service*. Enterprise services promote consistency of business policies across the company. They are large in scope and may be implemented as a complete system of services organized by business process flows. Figure 24 shows the various levels of services and how they support the basic technology of SOA.

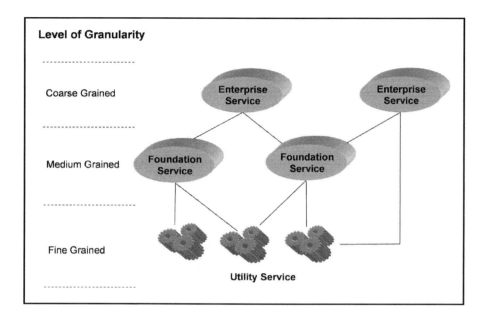

Figure 24—Service Hierarchy

This figure illustrates different types of services organized into a three level hierarchy. All three types of services use the same set of industry-accepted standards. However, they differ in the scope of work each can perform, as well as the business specific rules (policies) they can execute.

This example of a service hierarchy demonstrates that a specific set of policies should be established around services at each level. Since setting polices cannot be decentralized across the company, the enterprise architecture department is the best entity to set and maintain service policies. Enterprise architecture must determine the levels of granularity and set and enforce polices around services; otherwise, SOA will fail as an initiative.

A database and associated tools can make the SOA governance process more efficient and effective. As companies mature along the path toward SOA, enterprise architecture should employ a *service registry*. The service registry is a database where all services are documented. Tools associated with the registry enforce service policies and candidates for services can be standardized to assure they are reusable across lines of business. As services are developed, service governance procedures are required to avoid increasing support costs through uncontrolled service proliferation. Figure 25 shows the infrastructure required to manage services according to SOA best practices.

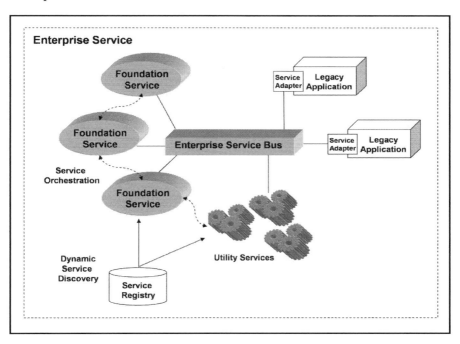

Figure 25—SOA Infrastructure

This figure shows the key elements of SOA technology. This new business process has been defined by management as an enterprise service. It includes access to two legacy applications. These applications were enhanced with service adapters to make them part of the enterprise service ecosystem. The enterprise service is formed by all components conforming to the integration standards presented through the ESB. Foundational services and utility services were created as part of the overall service context. Business rules were created to link services together in a workflow (shown as dashed lines). Service components were documented within the service registry. Information about services could be obtained at code deployment time, or at run time, depending on the service discovery policies set by the architecture department. Each SOA component is described in more detail below:

Service Adapter—All components rendered as services must conform to a set of interface description standards as specified by the W3C. These standards are called the web-services definition language (WSDL). WSDL is used to resolve both the logical and physical link semantics between service consumers and service providers. WSDL defines port types, operations parameters, message formats, data types, message bindings, and other details about service integration.

There is, in effect, a "service contract" between parties in the connection. Since all service interfaces are described with WSDL regardless of their level in the hierarchy, cross-platform integration can be standardized at the company level. Also, since many legacy systems may reside on the mainframe, additional gateway technology may be required to bridge distributed and mainframe-based platforms.

Enterprise Service Bus—The ESB is a core element in the SOA. As a logical entity, it is responsible for managing messaging between services. The ESB should support various types of messaging, including messaging using RMI over IIOP and indirect messaging using SOAP/XML with a store-and-forward transaction broker over native TCP/IP. The ESB is responsible for managing the quality of service (QoS) for messages and centralizes common functions of all services, such as message error handling.

The ESB is the transport mechanism for all reusable services in the company, regardless of whether RMI/IIOP or SOAP/XML is used to format messages. Experience shows that RMI/IIOP and RMI/http deliver the lowest message latency. When RMI is used to transfer messages between services, data can be transferred in virtual Java objects. Data transferred using virtual Java objects deliver lower response times because they do not require the same transformation processing required by XML. SOAP/XML should be used to meet loose-coupling requirements. SOAP/XML is independent of any programming language bindings or platform specifics. However, parsing of SOAP XML messages takes time, and will be some what slower (about 20 percent) than RMI using serialized Java objects.

Service Orchestration—There are times when foundational services need to execute in a specific sequence, or the underlying business transaction may be long-lived. The business rules say that the work is not completed until some later event occurs. In these cases, workflow technology is required. Typically, a workflow software product is used to coordinate the state of the business transaction between services. The W3C has defined a standard called business process execution language (BPEL) which, similar to WSDL, defines the semantics of the work to be shared or moved between services.

Using service orchestration, developers can combine lower level services into higher-level services leading to the enterprise service level. Developing the sophistication needed to combine services in this manner takes time for most organizations and is usually associated with a company that has reached a high level of maturity regarding the adoption of the SOA model.

Service Registry—The service registry is used to document the existence of all services in the enterprise. Registries can be active or passive. Active registries are called by services as they execute in real-time using UDDI as the standard interface protocol. This is called *dynamic service discovery*. Using this style of SOA, services can be generated in real time, and other services can be programmed to discover them during run time.

Since dynamic service discovery takes time, adding to transaction latency, many companies have opted not to implement UDDI. The alternative to UDDI is to leverage the registry during code-deployment time. Rules can be developed which require services to be logged in the registry before being migrated through the software distribution processes of the company. An offline service registry provides developers with a single location to find preexisting services. It can be used by enterprise architecture to measure the level of reuse of services across the company. Reports generated from the registry are useful when debugging problems with services. These reports list service owners and identify application-service dependencies.

SOA as the Enterprise Bridge

Figure 25 shows an example of how the major elements of SOA are used together to formulate a new architecture based on services. However, as SOA continues to mature, so too are three other major technologies. These are *business process management* (BPM), *business rules enablement* (BRE), and *content-document management* (CDM). Each of these areas evolved independently over the years, but now with SOA, are converging to bring new capabilities to the business. Each technical area has evolved through different vendor product offerings. Each software vendor, attempting to build more comprehensive solutions for customers has worked its way into the others' core competency. As each technology migrates into the others' primary market, managing the overlap becomes a challenge for I/T management. The figure below shows an example of how the three distinct areas intersect.

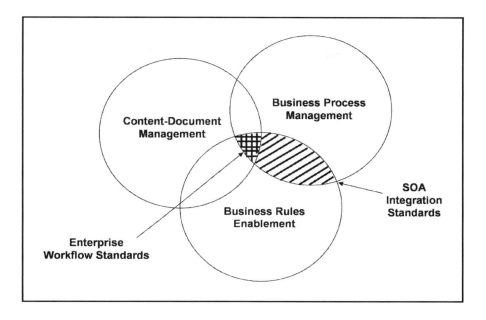

Figure 26—Enterprise Service Integration

Content-document management (CDM) is technology that scans, captures, indexes, and stores images of documents. Unstructured content, such as digital voiceprints, digital audio/video, text, and various graphic images are also being captured by many organizations. All this information can be placed into one or more repositories and used in day-to-day business processes. CDM vendors with roots in document imaging have developed workflow software to move images around the organization, creating overlap with other technologies targeted at workflow.

Business process management (BPM) is technology developed by vendors with roots in business process automation. Typically, this technology does not focus on scanning and indexing of documents or images, rather it is focused on managing long-running business transactions. This technology relies on databases that store work queues and usually contains a rules engine to "route" work to people across the enterprise. Many BPM solutions also incorporate business rule processing technology, creating overlap with rules management solutions.

Business rules enablement (BRE) matured from software that has its roots in the inference engine technology of the 1980s. Rules engines were first introduced as artificial intelligence (AI) solutions and have since evolved into sophisticated decision engines. BREs support changing business processing logic through rules and do not always require programming changes. This creates overlaps between the rules engines available from a BRE vendor and the rules engines used to route work that comes from vendors in the BPM business.

Using SOA, a business can follow a best-of-breed model for these three major software solutions. As long as each vendor within its respective domain follows SOA standards, the three solutions can interoperate. Resolving the overlapping technology problem is possible through the use of the ESB. The ESB can marshall data between software suites, guarantee delivery, and even manage the priorities of transactions.

The SOA/ESB approach supports purchased applications and in-house solutions that contain variations of these three functions. Enterprise architecture sets the interoperability standards at the enterprise level for these and the ARB acts as the governance body. The ARB evaluates vendor solutions for adherence to the enterprise-integration standards and any that do not follow standards are eliminated from consideration. For those that do not follow standards, special adapters are needed to include them as part of the company's technical ecosystem.

For example, a CRM solution may contain an embedded workflow solution, but to move work from within the CRM application to other databases or applications across the company, workflow elements would be brokered through the ESB. The ESB is responsible for assuring work elements are transported from the CRM to other systems without error. It assures they are converted from CRM specific formats into formats acceptable by receiving systems and vice versa.

Think of the system of rivers within a continent. Each continent would have its own system of rivers, but to get from one continent to the other, one must travel the ocean. Enterprise architecture establishes which technologies (or vendor products) represent the enterprise workflow system (the ocean). They define the interface specifications for the enterprise and govern how subordinate workflow applications connect to it (the port authority).

Evolution of SOA

As the underlying technology of SOA evolves, will the business adapt? Is SOA just "the next big thing," or will it become part of the overall landscape of computing over the long term? Forty years of software evolution is a very long time. Modular computing has been around since the dawn of programming. Even assembly language developed for the early IBM mainframes incorporated modularity as a concept. Assembler macros were, and are, a major part of the lowest level language used to program systems dating back to the 1960s. Modular programming concepts were applied to COBOL and PL/1. C++ and SmallTalk helped mature the modularity concept even more with the object-oriented programming model.

Then Java burst onto the scene, driving modularity to another level. Native Java was followed by the enterprise Java bean standards, and now we have SOA. The ideas behind SOA are not new. However, the combination of open standards and the stateless nature of applications developed for the web, create a new way for software to be packaged. Estimates of the benefits resulting from reusing software objects claim up to 80 percent savings in software development costs. These savings are net of the additional investment required to apply SOA technology to achieve high levels of reuse.

Engineers have always sought to build software that is platform independent, reusable, and interoperable. As more companies adopt WSDL, SOAP/XML, and the WS-standards, these goals are within reach. Even if the term SOA dies out, the standards behind

161

the term are likely to remain useful and will continue to evolve. The future of these standards is not in the hands of a single company or individual, but is advanced through a consortium of companies interested in furthering the state of the art. However, what remains to be seen is, will business leaders reorganize around a service model?

Enterprise Architecture can add significant value by helping the business understand the service model. A strong enterprise architecture function can drive the entire organization toward a service model. This process starts with an investment in the enterprise architecture repository. Once the application architecture is documented in the repository, analysis can be performed on the portfolio of applications. The head of enterprise architecture works closely with the CIO and various business leaders to determine which systems are core and which are not.

By linking costs associated with redundant and non-core business processes, significant cost reduction opportunities are identified. The key to moving an enterprise toward the service model is investing in SOA, starting small and documenting benefits associated with elimination of redundant systems. As redundant systems are eliminated, services are inserted into the application architecture, raising the level of business process flexibility. Cost reduction, savings from software reuse and improved business process flexibility make moving to a SOA a worthwhile endeavor.

Chapter 10—Summary

This chapter described the concept of a service-oriented architecture. A definition of SOA was provided followed by a description of the difference between a service-oriented strategy and the technology of SOA. The strategy of SOA was defined as a process that differentiates between core and non-core business processes. The chapter described an organizational structure for services based on the amount of business logic included within their design. The concept of the service-oriented enterprise was explored as a means to reduce operating expenses and improve business flexibility.

The technology of SOA was described and a summary of the major components that comprise the architecture were defined. The topic of technology convergence was raised and a method for resolving technical overlaps resulting from vendor provided software was presented. The chapter concluded with comments about the origin of SOA and how it will evolve in the future.

The following chapter discusses how the enterprise architecture function should be staffed and its reporting structure. It includes sample metrics that are useful in managing the function on a daily basis.

CHAPTER 11

Managing the Function

Few books about enterprise architecture talk about what it takes to successfully manage the function. Even fewer discuss how culture and politics affect the function. This chapter discusses targeting the organization charter, staffing the department, and developing management metrics.

Targeted Charter

Organizations need a mission statement and charter. What should the mission and charter be for enterprise architecture? The answer to this question depends on how the CIO views the function and where the function resides on the maturity curve discussed in chapter 1. The CIO could believe that enterprise architecture should be focused on setting standards and identifying cost reduction opportunities. Conversely, the CIO could believe the function should focus on evaluation of emerging technologies and innovation.

These two extremes are polar opposites. Each would require a different staffing model and different success criteria. The leader of Enterprise Architecture must understand how the CIO views the function, as well as what the culture of the business will accept. Are I/T and the business used to top-down direction, or is the company used to a consensus style of management? Is there a market leadership mentality or is the company a fast follower regarding technical innovation? To run a successful operation, the head of enterprise architecture needs to understand these parameters and factor them into the overall direction of the department. Figure 27 illustrates finding the correct position between the two extremes of being focused on standards or innovation.

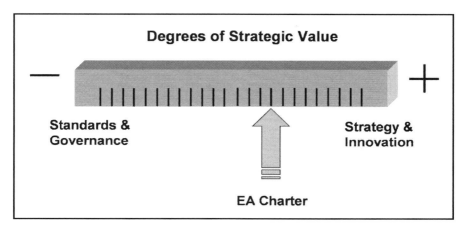

Figure 27—Positioning the Department

Using standards to enforce polices on a culture that normally works through consensus will not work very well. Also, why focus resources on developing a business strategy or evaluating emerging technology if the company is totally focused on the next quarter's financial results? Sometimes, with the appropriate support from the CIO and other upper management, enterprise architecture can become the change agent to encourage long term planning. If a company has been too focused on tactics, enterprise architecture can be the only department in I/T that has the time and resources available to evaluate emerging solutions. The leader of the architecture function must understand the overall context in which the department resides. This understanding will help to develop the best structure for the department and hire people with the correct skill set.

Let's look at the organization structure of enterprise architecture. How large should the department be, where should the department report, and what does the organization structure look like? In most cases, there are also other areas within I/T that perform what might be considered enterprise architecture department responsibilities. How should the structure account for "domain architects" or "application architects" that do not report to the head of enterprise architecture? As usual, the answer to these questions is "it depends."

The architecture department can be sized appropriately with an understanding of the overall role enterprise architecture plays within the broader scope of I/T. If enterprise architecture also runs the project management office (PMO) for I/T, then the department is likely to be as large as fifty or more resources. In the case where the PMO resides outside of architecture, the architecture staffing level is normally between fifteen and thirty people. To be effective in a large enterprise, (five hundred or more applications development personnel) the enterprise architecture department should be no smaller than fifteen people. Figure 28 provides a sample organization chart that assumes a balance is required between being focused on technical governance and I/T strategy.

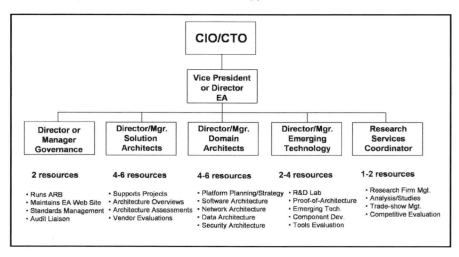

Figure 28—Sample EA Organization Structure

The sample organization chart shows the balance between resources applied to tactical work and strategic work. The left side of the chart shows the teams focused on governance.

Responsibilities include managing the ARB and maintaining standards and the architecture website. An architecture website is critical to maintaining awareness of the standards and best practices developed by the enterprise architecture department.

The sample organizational model assumes that a team of solution architects is centralized. These are experienced resources that help project teams with major initiatives that span the enterprise. These resources act like internal consultants and therefore must possess a broad spectrum of skills.

Depending on the overall philosophy of the CIO, the domain architects may also be centralized. These are people with a high degree of experience within specific major technical domains. The domains match to the overall architectural framework of the enterprise and include platforms, software (including middleware), network, data, and security. These resources could also be decentralized into various applications development or engineering groups within I/T. If domain architects are decentralized, at least two resources are needed within enterprise architecture to assure that each area is coordinated with the others across technical disciplines.

If enterprise architecture is responsible for evaluation of emerging technologies, then a team is needed to focus on execution of proof-of-architecture projects and productivity tool evaluations. A service can be created to manage various contracts and relationships with outside consulting agencies. These are typically companies focused on providing research, tracking I/T advancements, and in some cases, monitoring technology evolution within the company's industry.

There are leaders in each functional area within the architecture organization. Since the resources under each area are limited, a good practice is to assume the leadership positions are also working positions. Depending on the overall culture of the company, the leadership positions could be director or manager level positions. In either case, these leaders must work with senior leaders across I/T, the business and outside vendors. For this reason, to be effective, they must be people with senior titles granted the authority to make important recommendations and decisions on a daily basis.

In most companies there is considerable debate about whether standards are set by the respective domain areas or by the enterprise architecture department. The leader of enterprise architecture, working with the CIO or CTO, must be flexible and able to adapt to the culture. If there is a need to centralize, then the architecture team must take steps to assure there is buy-in for standards and assure that governance processes are followed. This is done by building partnerships with the business and I/T areas that control the allocation of funds to important projects.

If the culture believes in decentralized standards management, then the head of architecture must assure that there is one, and only one, official place where standards are documented and managed. The ARB, in this case, becomes the place where various opinions and viewpoints are worked out. However, it must be clear that the ARB is a function of enterprise architecture, and those that do not follow the collaborative review processes will not be able to move forward without obtaining a management consensus.

Staffing the Function

Staffing the enterprise architecture function is a challenge. To be effective, the group must have people who are respected for their technical knowledge and are able to communicate well using consensus and collaboration techniques. Finding people with the right combination of skills is difficult. Enterprise architects may require higher salaries as compared to other staff within I/T.

Winning the battle with the human resources department about salaries and reporting levels within the corporate hierarchy is possible through the use of industry benchmarks. Requesting that jobs be evaluated against similar roles in the same industry will help make the point about what type of people are needed within the architecture department. People working in the enterprise architecture department *are* different and here's why.

In baseball, professional scouts rate prospects according to a scale on five different dimensions. Players that score high on all five are called "five tool players." These include hitting, hitting for power, running speed, throwing strength, and fielding. In evaluating resources for enterprise architecture there are also five major dimensions to consider. These include program management, software architecture, data architecture, network architecture, and platform architecture. As figure 29 shows, an experience scale can be established for each dimension yielding a complete picture of a candidate. People with the highest level of attainment across all five dimensions would be "five tool players."

	Program Management	Software Architecture	Data Architecture	Network Architecture	Platform Architecture
Master (Level 5)	Leads enterprise wide Programs (multi-projects)	Defines long-term Enterprise software and middleware strategy	Determines logical and physical data direction for the company	Determines long term network and security direction	Determines long term hardware and O/S direction
Expert (Level 4)	Leads large projects Develops program plans	Sets standards, direction and best practices for software development	Establishes logical and physical data mgt. policies and direction	Establishes logical and physical network design and direction	Develops hardware refresh models and O/S migration plans
Leader (Level 3)	Assists with program Leadership, develops Program and project Plans	Leads others in use of standards and best practices	Determines platforms and recommends best practices	Manages network projects and Implementations	Develops hardware and O/S designs for major projects
Experienced (Level 2)	Supports other program Managers, develops project plans	Works with others on standards application and middleware use	Supports others with data access design and best practices	Supports network design and implementation	Supports hardware and O/S implementation
Novice (Level 1)	Assists project leaders maintains project plans	Assists with standards and product evaluations	Documents logical and physical data models	Documents logical and physical network architectures	Documents hardware and O/S standards and road-maps

Figure 29—Architecture Skill Set Dimensions

To be the most flexible in meeting the needs of the business and I/T, the head of enterprise architecture should strive for a good mix of resources covering the five dimensions. Resources that have achieved level 4 or level 5 across all of these would be the best candidates for the solution architect positions. These resources can do almost anything technical and are valuable across a wide array of enterprise-wide projects and initiatives.

Resources who have mastered a particular dimension, such as data architecture or network architecture, are best candidates for the domain architect positions. Software architecture is a broad dimension that includes software design, industry best practices, and middleware. Included within this area would be resources skilled in application development using various programming languages and design styles like object-oriented programming and SOA.

169

Below are some job descriptions for these resources. They are provided as samples because each company will have its own unique set.

Vice President/Director of Enterprise Architecture

This resource would normally have more than ten or fifteen years of experience depending on the circumstances of the organization. He or she would have experience with, and probably has mastered, all five of the key architecture skill set dimensions. The best resource is one with superior communication skills who is able to effect change across large and diverse organizations. The resource will also have experience within the industry in which the company competes. Leadership qualities are the most important aspect of this role, but having a technical background is also important. This person must be able to translate complex ideas, technology, and programs into language upper management can relate to. This person is a key influencer on technical decisions that affect the business on a long-term basis.

Director/Manger of Architecture Governance

This role is responsible for enterprise architecture standards and leads the Architecture Review Board (ARB). The resource coordinates approval for proposed architecture designs to ensure projects are aligned with standards and I/T strategy. He or she allocates appropriate resources to ensure that projects are completed within committed time and budget and are integrated with other I/T architecture projects. The role approves I/T architecture policies, standards, and procedures. This person is responsible for the enterprise architecture repository and for maintaining the architecture website and other communcation channels for the department.

Director/Manager of Solution Architects

This role acts as the ambassador for Enterprise Architecture to other teams within I/T. The person frequently meets with business leaders to understand and translate business direction into technology requirements. He or she prioritizes and assigns work to solution architects. The person leads the solution architects in development of common frameworks based on industry and enterprise architcture standards. He or she works closely with application development teams to help identify and define technical services that are candidates for reuse across the enterprise. The role mentors other members of I/T on the use of internally developed and externally procured software frameworks, tools, utilities, and objects. The resource works with others to establish the messaging standards across the enterprise and verifies that standards are applied to projects on a day-to-day basis.

Solution Architect

The Solution Architect completes work on large and complex IT architecture projects with full competency. The resource is responsible for the major architecture deliverables for enterprise-wide programs and line-of-business projects, including system designs and architecture blueprints. He or she engages domain architects regarding hardware engineering, data architecture, and software design best practices. The Solution Architect provides integrated systems planning and recommends innovative technologies that will enhance the current or proposed system designs. The resource recommends appropriate middleware and communication links required to support I/T goals and strategy and may coordinate the activities of the project team. Solution Architects assist in monitoring project schedules and costs when asked by project managers.

Director/Manager of Domain Architects

This resource is responsible for the integrity of designs provided by domain experts across I/T. He or she oversees and coordinates efforts across the various major practice areas of design, regardless of the resources being centralized or decentralized. He or she attends all ARB meetings and brokers solutions when disagreements arise regarding design options. The resource is responsible for raising issues to I/T management regarding conflicting or disconnected efforts across I/T. He or she is responsible for developing compromises and alternatives to resolve design conflicts at the enterprise level.

Director/Manager of Emerging Technology

The resource is assigned with keeping the I/T department current on technological advancements. The person leads proof-of-architecture (POA) projects to evaluate emerging technologies. He or she prepares business cases to justify the adoption of new technologies and assists with internal communcations leading to successful adoption of leading practices and technologies. The resource is a team member on formalized RFIs (request for information) conducted by other members within I/T and Enterprise Architecture. The person assists with preparation of RFI documentation and acts as lead documentation specialist/technical writer for various proof-of-concept (POC) efforts. The resource assists in development of communication plans for the enterprise architecture department.

Research Services Coordinator

This person acts as the single point of contact to the research firms on behalf of I/T and the business. He or she negotiates and manages research contracts with outside firms and responds to requests for research reports from within I/T and from the business. The resource prepares summaries of research information accumulated from various sources for management use. He or she keeps track of research firm utilization statistics and reports on the viability of vendor-provided services. The resource proactively seeks out new sources of information for management and produces periodic updates in newsletter style.

These are only samples of the types of jobs that may exist within the Enterprise Architecture department. Every company has a different view on the overall role of the department. However, by keeping the degree of strategic value desired by upper management in mind, the leader of enterpirse architecture will have developed the correct organization using the most appropriate resource mix to meet the needs of the company.

Knowing how well the department is doing and the ability to articulate value are also critical challenges for the leader of Enterprise Architecture. Since the department typically does not build systems or deliver business solutions, justifying the investment for the department is key to the long term success of the function. The following section provides a model for measuring the value of the architecture function.

Management Metrics

Because Enterprise Architecture is a staff function, meaning that it normally does not build things, developing meaningful metrics is difficult. However, by capturing the appropriate metrics, progress can be measured, value can be calculated and the group justified. The best way to develop metrics for a staff function like Enterprise Architecture is to analyze inputs and outputs. What work goes into the team and what deliverables come out? If the group is designed per the examples in this chapter, work will come into the group in the form of the following:

- requests for standards exceptions
- requests for architecture assessments
- requests for support on new projects
- vendor product evaluations
- requests for design reviews
- support with problem determination
- requests for long-term technical plans

Metrics describing work products coming out from Enterprise Architecture may include the following:

- number of system design documents reviewed
- number of standard exceptions granted

- number of architecture assessment documents created
- number of architecture blueprint documents created
- request for information or request for proposals supported
- value of systems retired
- value of innovative solutions deployed
- number of common services developed
- savings from common services utilized
- problems averted due to design recommendations

While these outputs can be measured, determing their value is difficult. One way to measure value of support services is to survey the customers. After each architecture service is completed, a survey can be sent out asking for input. Surveys can be written to measure if expectations were met on each engagement. A ranking system can be developed for survey results and the grades aggregated to generate a "customer satisfaction score."

As Enterprise Architecture documents systems within the enterprise repository, metrics about cost can be captured. How old are the applications? How many I/T resources support them? How much infrastructure do they consume (CPU cycles and storage)? All of these metrics can be factored into a formula that determines the real savings of eliminating legacy applications.

Enterprise Architecture can also lead efforts for server and data center consolidation. These projects normally yield large savings, clearly justifying the investment in the architecture function.

From a research support perspective, enterprise architecture can measure research firm usage and identify services that overlap across research vendors. The number of research firms can be consolidated to a few that provide the most benefit and firms that are not used often, or provide similar services to those that are used frequently, can be eliminated.

Enterprise Architecture is responsible for causing changes to occur across the company. As the architecture function matures, a track record can be maintained of new technology and solutions introduced by enterprise architecture over time. Figure 30 provides an example of how enterprise architecture impacts the company over time.

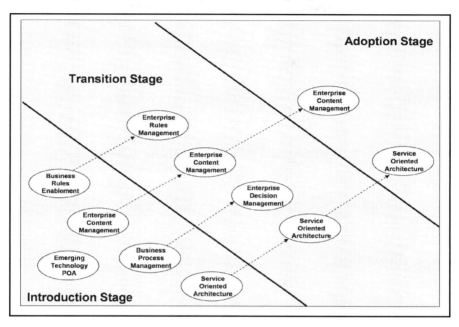

Figure 30—Enterprise Architecture Impact

This figure shows that new technology is introduced to the organization in three distinct stages. The *introduction stage* is led by the Enterprise Architecture team. Emerging technology is evaluated and tested. Standards and best practice documents are prepared for solutions that are determined to be important to I/T and the business. The architecture team is staffed with resources that are freed up of day-to-day issues, so they can work on evaluating and proving the viability of innovative solutions.

Applying new technology is not easy, as applications development and engineering groups are busy with company priorities. Therefore, it is the job of architecture to prove the new technology and become experts on it to assist with transition. During the *transition stage*, architecture provides expert assistance to project team members. The best way to move something new into the mainstream is by finding early adopters. These are people in need of innovative solutions to meet their goals. During the transition stage, Enterprise Architecture works in an advisory role, as the new technology is adopted by others in the organization.

Sometimes, letting go of a new and exciting solution is difficult for members of the architecture team, but they must; otherwise they will become a bottleneck to adoption at a later date. Once early adopters have experienced success they spread the word. Word-of-mouth about early success helps "sell" the new solutions to others. Soon, the new technology is being used by many groups and becomes mainstream to the organization in the *adoption stage*. Once the technology is completely transitioned, architecture need only track compliance to standards and recommended best practices. This adoption life cycle is perpetual and positive effects on the organization can be tracked and measured.

Chapter 11—Summary

Establishing the correct focus for the department is a challenge. So is hiring the right people. This chapter provided a methodology for determing the focus of the organization and then staffing the function accordingly. A sample organization chart was provided. A set of capabilities useful in talent evaluation was described along with criteria for evaluation of resources. This was followed by sample job descriptions. The chapter identified performance metrics that are useful in managing the architecture function. A model was provided that tracks innovative solutions from introduction through transition and mainstream adoption.

The following chapter provides a series of final thoughts summarizing the value Enterprise Architecture brings to companies.

CHAPTER 12

Final Thoughts

Each of the first three chapters of this book began with an analogy of a ship lost at sea. The captain and crew worked together to reach the safety and prosperity of the distant shore. While being lost at sea isn't the most positive analogy for a book about technology, for many, it smacks of reality. Businesses are always changing. They must change, to remain viable to their customers. Otherwise, they risk becoming irrelevant to their markets. As businesses evolve so too does information technology.

Technological evolution is chaotic, as there is no grand plan about what new products are brought to market. Nothing exemplifies this better than the rise of the Internet and all of the new ways people and businesses use it. Computing innovation seems to come about one I/T sector at a time. Computers evolve according to Moore's Law. Storage devices keep getting smaller and faster, networks are faster and cheaper, and software is open and sophisticated. Each facet of I/T changes at its own pace according to what vendors believe their customers want and need.

So how can I/T professionals keep up as business and I/T change simultaneously? Is there any chance of planning, or actually being out in front of the next set of business changes? This book provides a mechanism for being on target with long term plans. Chapter 1 provided a description of enterprise architecture and described what can happen if technological advances go unaddressed for too long. Chapter 2 offered a set of principles that can serve as guidelines for day-to-day decisions. Chapter 3 spoke of governance and how to manage change using consensus and empowered committees. These processes work best with a predetermined set of standards formed from the company culture, industry best practices, and open standards.

As the technologies in each I/T sector continue to evolve, the real magic is having the foresight to bring them together to formulate business solutions that make a difference. By understanding the trajectory of the architecture framework composed of application architecture, information architecture, network architecture, platform architecture and operations management architecture, the future is not as difficult to predict. The chapters in the mid section of the book focus on the components of the enterprise architecture framework. The layers of the framework work as a system to form the technology base present in all companies.

Applications have been implemented on top of one another for decades. Each new major technological innovation from the invention of the disk drive to the current Web-services interfaces has brought new capabilities to business. The challenge remains in finding ways of retiring older redundant technology while continuing to move forward. Applications today are actually running our major industries and many operational constraints are due to decade-old technology decisions. It is up to the Enterprise Architecture department within I/T to build the case for retiring older applications. Conversion plans must be carefully laid out, and investment cycles must match revenue streams for management to support such dramatic change.

Anything that can be digitized becomes information. Investment in information architecture has become a basic requirement for business to remain viable. Everyone is awash in data and trying to manage vast amounts of data without an "inventory control system" is futile. Artifacts like the corporate metadata repository, once optional for companies, are now needed to meet various regulatory requirements and to keep costs from spiraling out of control. Advances in database technology and supporting hardware make using terabytes of data the norm. The information architecture establishes policies for data use not only within the enterprise, but outside the enterprise as well. New technologies are available to effectively manage data through its life cycle. These help companies manage data at the lowest possible cost, while still meeting all access, security and recovery requirements.

Networking technology has also evolved dramatically over the years. Huge investments in fiber optic backbones have made ultra high-speed networking affordable to everyone, even to many homes around the world. At the same time, wireless networking has risen to a status equal to that of landline networks. Cellular, Wi-Fi, Wi-Max, Bluetooth, RFID and NFC have become part of daily life. Payment networks have also reached across the globe to enable commerce on a massive scale. It is likely these different network technologies will each continue to evolve at their own pace. However, new business opportunities exist on a grand scale by linking them together. New applications that bridge the Internet, cellular, and payment networks are beginning to emerge. Use of Wi-Fi, Bluetooth, RFID and NFC technologies are appearing in consumer products of all kinds. As homes continue to consume broadband and wireless services, new ways of reaching consumers will emerge. The network architecture is a good place to look when designing innovative new products for consumers.

Platforms have come and gone over the years. What remains, however, is a commitment by a few important worldwide vendors to stay focused on innovation. With so many choices of computing power today, picking the correct platform for the job at hand has become more challenging. Architects and engineers must reach agreement about platform differentiating requirements. Knowledge about transaction rates, memory utilization requirements, and I/O rates at design time, will improve the platform selection process. The key to platform selection and design is *balance*. Engineers must balance all aspects of the performance equation to be successful. Platform virtualization is a major advancement in platform architecture. By running virtual copies of the operating system, engineers can run systems closer to capacity than ever before, reducing costs and improving service.

Of course, no amount of innovation would be beneficial if the systems that run our companies were frequently unavailable or performing poorly. Because applications run our businesses and even save lives, they must be reliable. Poor reliability has been the bane of computing since the first systems were built in the 1950s. Over the years, almost everyone in I/T has worked to improve reliability. Reaching 100 percent availability is no small feat and, in many cases, isn't even cost-effective. However, it is important for a company to classify its applications according to a reliability scheme. Once a rating scheme is agreed upon, I/T can recommend architectures that meet availability requirements.

Since much of computer failure is induced by human error, procedures must be established. Processes like problem management, change management, asset management, and configuration management are all aimed at improving systems availability. Systems must be architected considering the time it takes to recover from failures. Business leaders and I/T management must be in agreement about recovery requirements so that I/T can effectively manage the investment in redundant systems.

What does the future have in store? Original concepts like program modularity have been reintroduced as the *service model*. Standards bodies are working on new open standards that enable service-oriented architecture. Upper management in today's enterprise is rethinking operations around a service model leading to the service-oriented enterprise.

Barriers of space and time are coming down to make the world into an "integrated work space." The enterprise architecture function, along with the talent that makes up the department, is poised to make its mark on business.

For the first time, business people are interested in systems architecture and what it can do to make everything easier to manage. Business agility has become a key element of sustainable success, while cost containment remains an important consideration. In a world where I/T work can be broken into small tasks and contracted out across many countries, architects and engineers are needed to bring everything together. The enterprise architecture function is one of the few areas in I/T with a comprehensive view across the enterprise and if leveraged appropriately, can drive business value on a huge scale.

INDEX

Index

Made in the USA